50 Walnut Wonder Recipes for Home

By: Kelly Johnson

Table of Contents

- Walnut Pesto Pasta
- Walnut and Blue Cheese Salad
- Walnut Crusted Chicken
- Walnut Banana Bread
- Maple Walnut Scones
- Walnut and Fig Tapenade
- Walnut-Crusted Salmon
- Walnut-Stuffed Mushrooms
- Walnut and Honey Tart
- Spicy Walnut Dip
- Walnut Brownies
- Walnut and Beet Salad
- Walnut Oatmeal Cookies
- Walnut and Apple Stuffing
- Caramel Walnut Pie
- Walnut and Kale Pesto
- Walnut Encrusted Pork Chops
- Walnut Bread
- Chocolate Walnut Fudge
- Walnut and Pear Salad
- Walnut and Cranberry Granola
- Spiced Walnut Loaf
- Walnut Chicken Salad
- Walnut Coffee Cake
- Walnut and Goat Cheese Crostini
- Walnut Pate
- Walnut and Roasted Red Pepper Spread
- Chocolate Walnut Biscotti
- Walnut and Quinoa Stuffed Peppers
- Walnut and Spinach Stuffed Chicken
- Walnut Chocolate Chip Cookies
- Walnut and Sun-Dried Tomato Pasta
- Walnut Blondies
- Walnut and Pumpkin Bread
- Walnut and Apricot Bites

- Walnut and Raspberry Bars
- Walnut, Date, and Coconut Balls
- Honey Walnut Shrimp
- Walnut and Cheese Stuffed Dates
- Roasted Walnut and Garlic Soup
- Walnut and Avocado Salad
- Cinnamon Walnut Pancakes
- Walnut and Rosemary Crackers
- Walnut and Orange Cake
- Spicy Walnut and Olive Tapenade
- Walnut and Carrot Cake
- Walnut and Lemon Biscotti
- Walnut and Herb Stuffed Tomatoes
- Walnut and Chocolate Truffles
- Walnut and Banana Smoothie

Walnut Pesto Pasta

Ingredients:

- For the Walnut Pesto:
    - 1 cup walnuts
    - 2 cups fresh basil leaves
    - 2 cloves garlic
    - 1/2 cup grated Parmesan cheese
    - 1/2 cup olive oil
    - Salt and pepper to taste
    - Juice of half a lemon (optional for brightness)
- For the Pasta:
    - 12 oz pasta (spaghetti, linguine, or your preferred type)
    - Salt for boiling pasta water
    - 1/4 cup reserved pasta water
    - Extra grated Parmesan cheese for serving
    - Fresh basil leaves for garnish

Instructions:

1. Prepare the Walnut Pesto:
    - In a dry skillet, toast the walnuts over medium heat until fragrant, about 5 minutes. Stir frequently to avoid burning. Let them cool.
    - In a food processor, combine the toasted walnuts, basil leaves, garlic, and Parmesan cheese. Pulse until the mixture is coarsely ground.
    - With the food processor running, slowly drizzle in the olive oil until the pesto reaches your desired consistency. You may need to scrape down the sides of the bowl once or twice.
    - Season with salt and pepper to taste. Add a squeeze of lemon juice if using.
2. Cook the Pasta:
    - Bring a large pot of salted water to a boil. Add the pasta and cook according to package instructions until al dente.
    - Reserve about 1/4 cup of the pasta cooking water, then drain the pasta.
3. Combine Pasta and Pesto:
    - In a large mixing bowl, toss the hot pasta with the walnut pesto. Add the reserved pasta water a little at a time to help coat the pasta evenly and to achieve a creamy consistency.
4. Serve:
    - Divide the pasta among serving plates.
    - Garnish with extra grated Parmesan cheese and fresh basil leaves.
    - Serve immediately and enjoy!

Tips:

- For a creamier texture, you can add a small amount of cream or ricotta cheese to the pesto.
- If you want a more intense basil flavor, use a combination of basil and parsley.
- Store any leftover pesto in an airtight container in the refrigerator for up to a week, or freeze it for longer storage.

Walnut and Blue Cheese Salad

Ingredients:

- For the Salad:
    - 6 cups mixed salad greens (such as arugula, spinach, and romaine)
    - 1 cup walnuts, toasted
    - 1/2 cup blue cheese, crumbled
    - 1 apple, thinly sliced (Granny Smith or Honeycrisp work well)
    - 1/2 red onion, thinly sliced
    - 1/2 cup dried cranberries or cherries
- For the Dressing:
    - 1/4 cup olive oil
    - 2 tablespoons apple cider vinegar
    - 1 tablespoon honey or maple syrup
    - 1 teaspoon Dijon mustard
    - Salt and pepper to taste

Instructions:

1. Prepare the Walnuts:
    - In a dry skillet, toast the walnuts over medium heat until fragrant, about 5 minutes. Stir frequently to avoid burning. Let them cool.
2. Make the Dressing:
    - In a small bowl, whisk together the olive oil, apple cider vinegar, honey (or maple syrup), Dijon mustard, salt, and pepper until well combined.
3. Assemble the Salad:
    - In a large salad bowl, combine the mixed salad greens, toasted walnuts, blue cheese, apple slices, red onion, and dried cranberries (or cherries).
4. Dress the Salad:
    - Drizzle the dressing over the salad and toss gently to combine, ensuring all the ingredients are evenly coated.
5. Serve:
    - Divide the salad among serving plates and enjoy immediately.

Tips:

- For added flavor, you can lightly candy the walnuts by tossing them in a skillet with a tablespoon of sugar and a pinch of salt until the sugar melts and coats the nuts.
- Pears can be used instead of apples for a different fruity twist.
- If you prefer a creamier dressing, you can add a tablespoon of mayonnaise or Greek yogurt to the dressing mixture.
- This salad pairs well with grilled chicken or steak for a more substantial meal.

Walnut Crusted Chicken

Ingredients:

- 4 boneless, skinless chicken breasts
- 1 cup walnuts, finely chopped
- 1/2 cup breadcrumbs (panko or regular)
- 1/2 cup grated Parmesan cheese
- 1/4 cup fresh parsley, chopped
- 2 cloves garlic, minced
- 1 teaspoon dried thyme
- 1/2 teaspoon salt
- 1/2 teaspoon black pepper
- 1/4 cup flour
- 1 egg, beaten
- 2 tablespoons olive oil

Instructions:

1. Preheat the Oven:
   - Preheat your oven to 375°F (190°C). Line a baking sheet with parchment paper or lightly grease it.
2. Prepare the Walnut Coating:
   - In a shallow bowl, combine the finely chopped walnuts, breadcrumbs, Parmesan cheese, parsley, minced garlic, dried thyme, salt, and black pepper. Mix well to combine.
3. Prepare the Chicken:
   - Pat the chicken breasts dry with paper towels. Lightly coat each chicken breast with flour, shaking off any excess.
4. Coat the Chicken:
   - Dip each floured chicken breast into the beaten egg, ensuring it is fully coated.
   - Press the chicken into the walnut mixture, pressing down firmly to ensure the coating adheres well to both sides of the chicken.
5. Cook the Chicken:
   - In a large skillet, heat the olive oil over medium-high heat.
   - Add the walnut-crusted chicken breasts to the skillet and cook for 2-3 minutes on each side, or until the crust is golden brown. You may need to do this in batches to avoid overcrowding the pan.
   - Transfer the browned chicken breasts to the prepared baking sheet.
6. Bake the Chicken:
   - Place the baking sheet in the preheated oven and bake for 15-20 minutes, or until the chicken is cooked through and reaches an internal temperature of 165°F (74°C).
7. Serve:

- Remove the chicken from the oven and let it rest for a few minutes before serving.
- Serve the walnut-crusted chicken with your favorite sides, such as roasted vegetables, mashed potatoes, or a fresh salad.

Tips:

- For an extra flavor boost, marinate the chicken breasts in a mixture of olive oil, lemon juice, and your favorite herbs for at least 30 minutes before coating.
- If you prefer a spicier dish, add a pinch of cayenne pepper or paprika to the walnut mixture.
- Leftover walnut-crusted chicken can be stored in an airtight container in the refrigerator for up to 3 days. Reheat in the oven to maintain the crispy texture.

Walnut Banana Bread

Ingredients:

- 1 3/4 cups all-purpose flour
- 1 teaspoon baking soda
- 1/2 teaspoon salt
- 1 teaspoon ground cinnamon (optional)
- 1/2 cup unsalted butter, melted and slightly cooled
- 1 cup granulated sugar
- 2 large eggs, at room temperature
- 1 teaspoon vanilla extract
- 1/2 cup plain Greek yogurt or sour cream
- 3 ripe bananas, mashed (about 1 1/2 cups)
- 1 cup walnuts, chopped

Instructions:

1. Preheat the Oven:
    - Preheat your oven to 350°F (175°C). Grease and flour a 9x5-inch loaf pan, or line it with parchment paper.
2. Prepare the Dry Ingredients:
    - In a medium bowl, whisk together the flour, baking soda, salt, and ground cinnamon (if using). Set aside.
3. Prepare the Wet Ingredients:
    - In a large bowl, whisk the melted butter and granulated sugar together until well combined.
    - Add the eggs, one at a time, beating well after each addition.
    - Stir in the vanilla extract and Greek yogurt (or sour cream) until smooth.
    - Mix in the mashed bananas until well incorporated.
4. Combine the Wet and Dry Ingredients:
    - Gradually add the dry ingredient mixture to the wet ingredients, stirring gently until just combined. Do not overmix.
    - Fold in the chopped walnuts.
5. Bake the Bread:
    - Pour the batter into the prepared loaf pan and spread it out evenly.
    - Bake in the preheated oven for 60-70 minutes, or until a toothpick inserted into the center of the bread comes out clean.
    - If the top of the bread starts to brown too quickly, cover it loosely with aluminum foil.
6. Cool and Serve:
    - Remove the bread from the oven and let it cool in the pan for about 10 minutes.
    - Transfer the bread to a wire rack to cool completely before slicing.

Tips:

- For added flavor, you can toast the walnuts in a dry skillet over medium heat for a few minutes before adding them to the batter.
- If you prefer a sweeter bread, add an extra 1/4 cup of granulated sugar or replace some of the sugar with brown sugar for a richer taste.
- You can also add chocolate chips or dried fruit (such as raisins or cranberries) to the batter for a different twist.
- Store any leftover banana bread in an airtight container at room temperature for up to 3 days, or wrap it tightly and freeze for up to 3 months.

Maple Walnut Scones

Ingredients:

- For the Scones:
    - 2 cups all-purpose flour
    - 1/4 cup granulated sugar
    - 1 tablespoon baking powder
    - 1/2 teaspoon salt
    - 1/2 cup unsalted butter, cold and cut into small cubes
    - 1/2 cup chopped walnuts
    - 1/2 cup heavy cream, plus more for brushing
    - 1/4 cup maple syrup
    - 1 teaspoon vanilla extract
    - 1 large egg
- For the Maple Glaze:
    - 1 cup powdered sugar
    - 3 tablespoons maple syrup
    - 1-2 tablespoons milk or cream

Instructions:

1. Preheat the Oven:
    - Preheat your oven to 400°F (200°C). Line a baking sheet with parchment paper or a silicone baking mat.
2. Prepare the Dry Ingredients:
    - In a large bowl, whisk together the flour, granulated sugar, baking powder, and salt.
3. Cut in the Butter:
    - Add the cold, cubed butter to the flour mixture. Using a pastry cutter or your fingers, cut the butter into the flour until the mixture resembles coarse crumbs. Stir in the chopped walnuts.
4. Mix the Wet Ingredients:
    - In a separate bowl, whisk together the heavy cream, maple syrup, vanilla extract, and egg until well combined.
5. Combine Wet and Dry Ingredients:
    - Pour the wet ingredients into the dry ingredients. Stir gently with a spatula or wooden spoon until just combined. Do not overmix.
6. Shape the Dough:
    - Turn the dough out onto a lightly floured surface and knead it gently a few times until it comes together. Pat the dough into a circle about 1 inch thick and 8 inches in diameter.
    - Cut the dough into 8 wedges and place them on the prepared baking sheet, spacing them slightly apart.
7. Bake the Scones:

- Brush the tops of the scones with a little heavy cream for a golden finish.
- Bake in the preheated oven for 15-18 minutes, or until the scones are golden brown and a toothpick inserted into the center comes out clean.

8. Prepare the Maple Glaze:
   - While the scones are baking, make the glaze. In a small bowl, whisk together the powdered sugar, maple syrup, and 1-2 tablespoons of milk or cream until smooth. Adjust the consistency as needed.
9. Glaze the Scones:
   - Allow the scones to cool for a few minutes on a wire rack. Drizzle the maple glaze over the warm scones.
10. Serve:
    - Serve the scones warm or at room temperature. Enjoy!

Tips:

- For extra flavor, you can toast the walnuts before adding them to the dough.
- If you prefer a stronger maple flavor, you can add a teaspoon of maple extract to the glaze.
- Scones are best enjoyed fresh but can be stored in an airtight container at room temperature for up to 2 days. Reheat them in the oven to regain their crispness if desired.

Walnut and Fig Tapenade

Ingredients:

- 1 cup dried figs, stems removed
- 1 cup walnuts, toasted
- 1/4 cup kalamata olives, pitted
- 2 tablespoons capers, drained
- 2 cloves garlic, minced
- 2 tablespoons fresh lemon juice
- 1 tablespoon balsamic vinegar
- 1/4 cup olive oil
- 1 teaspoon fresh thyme leaves (or 1/2 teaspoon dried thyme)
- Salt and pepper to taste

Instructions:

1. Prepare the Figs:
    - Place the dried figs in a bowl and cover with hot water. Let them soak for about 10 minutes to soften. Drain the figs and pat them dry with paper towels.
2. Toast the Walnuts:
    - In a dry skillet, toast the walnuts over medium heat until they are fragrant and lightly browned, about 5 minutes. Stir frequently to prevent burning. Let them cool.
3. Combine Ingredients:
    - In a food processor, combine the soaked figs, toasted walnuts, kalamata olives, capers, minced garlic, fresh lemon juice, and balsamic vinegar.
4. Process the Tapenade:
    - Pulse the mixture until it is coarsely chopped. With the food processor running, slowly drizzle in the olive oil until the mixture comes together and reaches your desired consistency. You may need to scrape down the sides of the bowl a few times to ensure everything is well mixed.
5. Season and Finish:
    - Add the fresh thyme leaves, and season with salt and pepper to taste. Pulse a few more times to combine.
6. Serve:
    - Transfer the tapenade to a serving bowl. It can be served immediately or refrigerated for a couple of hours to allow the flavors to meld.
    - Serve the walnut and fig tapenade with crusty bread, crackers, or as a condiment for sandwiches and grilled meats.

Tips:

- For a bit of heat, you can add a pinch of red pepper flakes to the tapenade.

- If the tapenade is too thick, you can thin it out with a little more olive oil or a splash of water.
- This tapenade can be stored in an airtight container in the refrigerator for up to a week.

Walnut-Crusted Salmon

Ingredients:

- 4 salmon fillets, skin-on or skinless (about 6 oz each)
- 1 cup walnuts, finely chopped
- 1/2 cup panko breadcrumbs
- 1/4 cup grated Parmesan cheese
- 2 tablespoons fresh parsley, finely chopped
- 1 tablespoon Dijon mustard
- 1 tablespoon honey
- 1 tablespoon olive oil
- Salt and pepper to taste
- Lemon wedges, for serving

Instructions:

1. Preheat the Oven:
    - Preheat your oven to 400°F (200°C). Line a baking sheet with parchment paper or lightly grease it.
2. Prepare the Walnut Crust:
    - In a bowl, combine the finely chopped walnuts, panko breadcrumbs, grated Parmesan cheese, and chopped fresh parsley. Season with salt and pepper to taste.
3. Prepare the Salmon:
    - Pat the salmon fillets dry with paper towels. If using skin-on salmon, place the fillets skin-side down on the prepared baking sheet.
4. Mix the Mustard-Honey Glaze:
    - In a small bowl, whisk together the Dijon mustard, honey, and olive oil until smooth.
5. Coat the Salmon:
    - Brush the top (non-skin side if using skin-on) of each salmon fillet with the mustard-honey glaze.
6. Apply the Walnut Crust:
    - Press the walnut mixture evenly onto the glazed side of each salmon fillet, coating it generously.
7. Bake the Salmon:
    - Bake in the preheated oven for 12-15 minutes, or until the salmon is cooked through and flakes easily with a fork. The crust should be golden and crispy.
8. Serve:
    - Remove the walnut-crusted salmon from the oven and let it rest for a couple of minutes.
    - Serve warm with lemon wedges on the side for squeezing over the salmon.

Tips:

- If you prefer a thicker crust, press the walnut mixture more firmly onto the salmon before baking.
- Adjust the baking time depending on the thickness of your salmon fillets. Thinner fillets will cook faster, while thicker fillets may need a few extra minutes.
- This walnut-crusted salmon pairs well with steamed vegetables, rice, or a fresh green salad for a complete meal.

Walnut-Stuffed Mushrooms

Ingredients:

- 16 large button mushrooms, stems removed and reserved
- 1/2 cup walnuts, finely chopped
- 1/2 cup breadcrumbs (panko or regular)
- 1/4 cup grated Parmesan cheese
- 2 cloves garlic, minced
- 2 tablespoons fresh parsley, finely chopped
- 1 tablespoon olive oil
- Salt and pepper to taste
- Cooking spray or olive oil for greasing

Instructions:

1. Prepare the Mushrooms:
    - Preheat your oven to 375°F (190°C). Grease a baking dish or line it with parchment paper.
    - Clean the mushrooms with a damp cloth to remove any dirt. Remove the stems from the mushrooms and finely chop them. Set the mushroom caps aside.
2. Prepare the Filling:
    - In a skillet, heat the olive oil over medium heat. Add the chopped mushroom stems and minced garlic. Cook for 3-4 minutes, until softened.
    - Add the finely chopped walnuts to the skillet and toast them for 2-3 minutes, stirring frequently.
    - Remove the skillet from heat and transfer the mixture to a bowl. Let it cool slightly.
3. Assemble the Filling:
    - To the bowl with the mushroom stems and walnuts, add the breadcrumbs, grated Parmesan cheese, chopped parsley, salt, and pepper. Mix everything together until well combined.
4. Stuff the Mushrooms:
    - Spoon the walnut mixture into each mushroom cap, pressing gently to fill them evenly and compactly.
5. Bake the Stuffed Mushrooms:
    - Place the stuffed mushrooms in the prepared baking dish. Lightly spray or brush the tops with olive oil.
    - Bake in the preheated oven for 20-25 minutes, or until the mushrooms are tender and the tops are golden brown.
6. Serve:
    - Remove the stuffed mushrooms from the oven and let them cool slightly before serving.
    - Garnish with additional chopped parsley if desired, and serve warm as a delicious appetizer or side dish.

Tips:

- You can customize the filling by adding diced cooked bacon or sausage for a meaty variation.
- For a vegetarian option, omit the Parmesan cheese or use a plant-based alternative.
- These walnut-stuffed mushrooms can be prepared ahead of time and baked just before serving. Cover and refrigerate them after assembling, then bake as directed when ready to serve.

Walnut and Honey Tart

Ingredients:

For the Tart Crust:

- 1 1/4 cups all-purpose flour
- 1/4 cup granulated sugar
- 1/2 teaspoon salt
- 1/2 cup unsalted butter, cold and cut into small pieces
- 1 large egg yolk
- 1-2 tablespoons ice water

For the Filling:

- 1 cup walnuts, chopped
- 1/2 cup honey
- 1/4 cup unsalted butter, melted
- 1/4 cup granulated sugar
- 2 large eggs
- 1 teaspoon vanilla extract
- Pinch of salt

Instructions:

1. Prepare the Tart Crust:
    - In a large bowl, whisk together the flour, sugar, and salt.
    - Add the cold butter pieces and cut into the flour mixture using a pastry cutter or your fingers, until the mixture resembles coarse crumbs.
    - In a small bowl, whisk together the egg yolk and 1 tablespoon of ice water. Gradually add this mixture to the flour-butter mixture, stirring with a fork, until the dough begins to come together. Add more ice water, 1 teaspoon at a time, if needed.
    - Turn the dough out onto a lightly floured surface and knead gently until it forms a ball. Flatten into a disk, wrap in plastic wrap, and refrigerate for at least 30 minutes.
2. Preheat the Oven:
    - Preheat your oven to 350°F (175°C). Lightly grease a 9-inch tart pan with a removable bottom.
3. Roll Out and Line the Tart Pan:
    - On a lightly floured surface, roll out the chilled dough into a circle slightly larger than your tart pan. Carefully transfer the dough to the tart pan and press it into the bottom and sides. Trim any excess dough from the edges.
4. Prepare the Filling:

- In a medium bowl, combine the chopped walnuts, honey, melted butter, sugar, eggs, vanilla extract, and a pinch of salt. Mix until well combined.
5. Assemble and Bake:
    - Pour the walnut-honey filling into the prepared tart crust, spreading it evenly.
    - Place the tart pan on a baking sheet (to catch any drips) and bake in the preheated oven for 30-35 minutes, or until the filling is set and the crust is golden brown.
6. Cool and Serve:
    - Remove the tart from the oven and let it cool in the pan on a wire rack for about 10 minutes.
    - Carefully remove the tart from the pan and let it cool completely on the wire rack before slicing and serving.
7. Optional Garnish:
    - Optionally, you can garnish the cooled tart with a drizzle of extra honey and a sprinkle of chopped walnuts before serving.
8. Serve and Enjoy:
    - Serve the walnut and honey tart at room temperature. It can be enjoyed on its own or with a dollop of whipped cream or a scoop of vanilla ice cream.

Tips:

- Make sure the tart crust is well chilled before rolling it out to prevent it from sticking.
- If you prefer a more pronounced honey flavor, you can increase the amount of honey in the filling.
- Store any leftovers in an airtight container in the refrigerator for up to 3 days.

Spicy Walnut Dip

- d
- 1 teaspoon ground cumin
- 1/2 teaspoon paprika
- 1/4 teaspoon cayenne pepper (adjust to taste for spiciness)
- Salt and pepper, to taste
- 1/4 cup plain Greek yogurt (optional, for creaminess)
- 2 tablespoons chopped fresh parsley or cilantro, for garnish

Instructions:

1. Toast the Walnuts:
    - In a dry skillet over medium heat, toast the walnuts until fragrant and lightly browned, stirring frequently to prevent burning. This should take about 5 minutes. Let them cool slightly.
2. Prepare the Dip:

- In a food processor, combine the toasted walnuts, olive oil, lemon juice, minced garlic, ground cumin, paprika, and cayenne pepper. Pulse until the mixture becomes a coarse paste.
3. Adjust Consistency:
   - If you prefer a creamier dip, add the Greek yogurt to the food processor and pulse until well combined. Adjust the thickness by adding a little more olive oil if needed.
4. Season to Taste:
   - Taste the dip and season with salt and pepper according to your preference. Adjust the spiciness by adding more cayenne pepper if desired.
5. Serve:
   - Transfer the spicy walnut dip to a serving bowl. Garnish with chopped fresh parsley or cilantro.
6. Enjoy:
   - Serve the dip with your choice of sliced vegetables (such as carrots, cucumbers, and bell peppers), pita bread, or use it as a spread for sandwiches and wraps.

Tips:

- You can customize this dip by adding other spices or herbs such as coriander, smoked paprika, or fresh mint.
- For a nuttier flavor, you can use a combination of walnuts and almonds or pecans.
- Store any leftovers in an airtight container in the refrigerator for up to 4 days. Stir well before serving again.

This dip is versatile and adds a deliciously spicy kick to any appetizer spread or meal!

Walnut Brownies

Ingredients:

- 1/2 cup unsalted butter
- 1 cup granulated sugar
- 2 large eggs
- 1 teaspoon vanilla extract
- 1/3 cup unsweetened cocoa powder
- 1/2 cup all-purpose flour
- 1/4 teaspoon salt
- 1/4 teaspoon baking powder
- 1/2 cup walnuts, chopped (plus extra for topping, if desired)
- Optional: 1/2 cup chocolate chips for extra chocolatey goodness

Instructions:

1. Preheat the Oven:
    - Preheat your oven to 350°F (175°C). Grease or line an 8x8-inch baking pan with parchment paper.
2. Melt the Butter:
    - In a medium-sized microwave-safe bowl, melt the butter in the microwave in 30-second intervals until fully melted.
3. Mix Wet Ingredients:
    - Stir in the granulated sugar, eggs, and vanilla extract into the melted butter until well combined.
4. Add Dry Ingredients:
    - Sift the cocoa powder, all-purpose flour, salt, and baking powder into the wet mixture. Stir until just combined. Do not overmix.
5. Fold in Walnuts and Chocolate Chips:
    - Gently fold in the chopped walnuts (and chocolate chips if using) into the brownie batter.
6. Bake:
    - Pour the batter into the prepared baking pan, spreading it out evenly with a spatula. Sprinkle additional chopped walnuts on top, if desired.
    - Bake in the preheated oven for 20-25 minutes, or until a toothpick inserted into the center comes out with a few moist crumbs (not wet batter).
7. Cool and Serve:
    - Allow the brownies to cool completely in the pan on a wire rack before slicing into squares.
8. Enjoy:
    - Serve the walnut brownies as they are, or with a scoop of vanilla ice cream for an extra treat!

Tips:

- Be careful not to overbake the brownies, as they can become dry. It's better to slightly underbake them for a fudgy texture.
- You can substitute walnuts with other nuts like pecans or almonds if desired.
- Store leftover brownies in an airtight container at room temperature for up to 3 days, or refrigerate for longer storage. Heat briefly in the microwave before serving to regain their fudgy texture.

Walnut and Beet Salad

Ingredients:

- 4 medium beets, cooked, peeled, and sliced into wedges
- 1/2 cup walnuts, toasted and chopped
- 4 cups mixed salad greens (such as arugula, baby spinach, and/or mixed greens)
- 1/4 cup crumbled feta cheese (optional)
- 1/4 cup red onion, thinly sliced
- 1/4 cup fresh parsley, chopped

For the Dressing:

- 1/4 cup extra virgin olive oil
- 2 tablespoons balsamic vinegar
- 1 tablespoon honey or maple syrup
- 1 teaspoon Dijon mustard
- Salt and pepper, to taste

Instructions:

1. Prepare the Beets:
    - If the beets are not already cooked, you can roast or boil them until tender. Let them cool, then peel and slice them into wedges.
2. Toast the Walnuts:
    - In a dry skillet over medium heat, toast the walnuts until fragrant and lightly browned, about 5 minutes. Stir frequently to prevent burning. Let them cool, then chop them.
3. Make the Dressing:
    - In a small bowl, whisk together the olive oil, balsamic vinegar, honey or maple syrup, Dijon mustard, salt, and pepper until well combined.
4. Assemble the Salad:
    - In a large salad bowl, combine the mixed salad greens, sliced beets, toasted walnuts, crumbled feta cheese (if using), sliced red onion, and chopped parsley.
5. Dress the Salad:
    - Drizzle the dressing over the salad and toss gently to coat everything evenly.
6. Serve:
    - Divide the salad among serving plates or bowls.
7. Optional Garnish:
    - You can sprinkle some extra crumbled feta cheese and a few additional chopped walnuts or parsley on top for garnish, if desired.
8. Enjoy:
    - Serve the walnut and beet salad immediately as a delicious and nutritious side dish or light main course.

Tips:

- To save time, you can often find pre-cooked and peeled beets in the produce section of many grocery stores.
- This salad can be made ahead of time. Keep the dressing separate until ready to serve to keep the salad fresh and crisp.
- Adjust the sweetness of the dressing by varying the amount of honey or maple syrup according to your preference.

Walnut Oatmeal Cookies

Ingredients:

- 1 cup unsalted butter, softened
- 1 cup packed brown sugar
- 1/2 cup granulated sugar
- 2 large eggs
- 1 teaspoon vanilla extract
- 1 1/2 cups all-purpose flour
- 1 teaspoon baking soda
- 1/2 teaspoon salt
- 3 cups old-fashioned rolled oats
- 1 cup walnuts, chopped
- Optional: 1/2 cup chocolate chips or raisins for extra flavor (if desired)

Instructions:

1. Preheat the Oven:
   - Preheat your oven to 350°F (175°C). Line baking sheets with parchment paper or silicone baking mats.
2. Cream Butter and Sugars:
   - In a large bowl, cream together the softened butter, brown sugar, and granulated sugar until light and fluffy using a hand mixer or stand mixer.
3. Add Eggs and Vanilla:
   - Beat in the eggs one at a time, then stir in the vanilla extract.
4. Combine Dry Ingredients:
   - In a separate bowl, whisk together the flour, baking soda, and salt.
5. Mix the Dough:
   - Gradually add the flour mixture to the creamed butter and sugar mixture, mixing until just combined.
6. Add Oats and Walnuts:
   - Stir in the rolled oats and chopped walnuts (and chocolate chips or raisins if using) until evenly distributed in the dough.
7. Form Cookies:
   - Drop rounded tablespoons of dough onto the prepared baking sheets, spacing them about 2 inches apart.
8. Bake:
   - Bake in the preheated oven for 10-12 minutes, or until the edges are lightly golden brown.
9. Cool:
   - Allow the cookies to cool on the baking sheets for a few minutes before transferring them to wire racks to cool completely.
10. Enjoy:

- Once cooled, serve these delicious walnut oatmeal cookies with a glass of milk or store them in an airtight container for later enjoyment!

Tips:

- For extra chewiness, you can refrigerate the cookie dough for 30 minutes to 1 hour before baking.
- Feel free to customize these cookies by adding other mix-ins like dried cranberries, coconut flakes, or white chocolate chips.
- These cookies also freeze well. Once completely cooled, store them in a freezer-safe container or bag for up to 3 months.

Walnut and Apple Stuffing

Ingredients:

- 8 cups bread cubes (about 1 loaf of bread, cut into cubes and dried out)
- 1/2 cup unsalted butter
- 1 large onion, diced
- 2 stalks celery, diced
- 2 apples (such as Granny Smith), cored and diced
- 1 cup chopped walnuts, toasted
- 2 teaspoons dried sage (or 2 tablespoons fresh sage, chopped)
- 1 teaspoon dried thyme
- 1/2 teaspoon dried rosemary
- Salt and pepper, to taste
- 1-2 cups chicken or vegetable broth
- 1/2 cup chopped fresh parsley
- Optional: 1/2 cup dried cranberries or raisins

Instructions:

1. Prepare the Bread Cubes:
    - If your bread cubes are not already dried out, spread them on a baking sheet and bake in a 300°F (150°C) oven for about 15-20 minutes, or until they are dry and slightly toasted. Set aside.
2. Preheat the Oven:
    - Preheat your oven to 350°F (175°C). Grease a 9x13-inch baking dish or a large oven-safe skillet.
3. Saute the Vegetables and Apples:
    - In a large skillet or saucepan, melt the butter over medium heat. Add the diced onion and celery, and cook until softened, about 5-7 minutes.
    - Add the diced apples and continue to cook for another 3-4 minutes, until the apples are slightly tender.
4. Combine Ingredients:
    - In a large bowl, combine the dried bread cubes, sautéed vegetables and apples, toasted walnuts, dried sage, thyme, rosemary, salt, and pepper. Toss everything together until well mixed.
5. Add Broth:
    - Gradually pour the chicken or vegetable broth over the bread mixture, stirring gently to moisten the bread cubes. Start with 1 cup of broth and add more as needed until the stuffing reaches your desired moistness. The amount of broth needed can vary based on how dry your bread cubes are.
6. Mix in Parsley and Optional Ingredients:
    - Stir in the chopped fresh parsley and dried cranberries or raisins (if using), distributing them evenly throughout the stuffing mixture.
7. Bake the Stuffing:

- Transfer the stuffing mixture to the prepared baking dish or skillet, spreading it out evenly.
- Cover the dish with aluminum foil and bake in the preheated oven for 30 minutes. Then, remove the foil and bake for an additional 15-20 minutes, or until the top is golden brown and crispy.

8. Serve:
    - Remove the stuffing from the oven and let it cool slightly before serving alongside your favorite poultry dish.

Tips:

- For a vegetarian version, use vegetable broth instead of chicken broth.
- Adjust the seasoning to your taste preferences. You can add more herbs or spices like cinnamon or nutmeg for additional flavor.
- Leftover stuffing can be stored in an airtight container in the refrigerator for up to 3-4 days. Reheat before serving.

Caramel Walnut Pie

Ingredients:

For the Pie Crust:

- 1 1/4 cups all-purpose flour
- 1/2 teaspoon salt
- 1/2 cup unsalted butter, cold and cut into cubes
- 3-4 tablespoons ice water

For the Filling:

- 1 cup granulated sugar
- 1/4 cup water
- 1/2 cup heavy cream
- 2 tablespoons unsalted butter
- 1/2 teaspoon vanilla extract
- 2 cups walnuts, toasted and chopped

Instructions:

1. Prepare the Pie Crust:
    - In a large bowl, whisk together the flour and salt. Add the cold cubed butter.
    - Using a pastry cutter or your fingers, work the butter into the flour mixture until it resembles coarse crumbs with pea-sized pieces of butter.
    - Gradually add the ice water, 1 tablespoon at a time, mixing gently with a fork until the dough comes together. Be careful not to overwork the dough.
    - Shape the dough into a disk, wrap it in plastic wrap, and refrigerate for at least 1 hour.
2. Preheat the Oven:
    - Preheat your oven to 375°F (190°C).
3. Roll Out the Dough:
    - On a lightly floured surface, roll out the chilled dough into a circle large enough to fit into a 9-inch pie dish. Carefully transfer the dough to the pie dish, pressing it gently into the bottom and sides. Trim any excess dough and crimp the edges decoratively.
4. Prepare the Caramel Filling:
    - In a medium saucepan, combine the granulated sugar and water over medium heat. Stir until the sugar dissolves.
    - Once the sugar has dissolved, stop stirring and allow the mixture to boil. Continue cooking, swirling the pan occasionally, until the mixture turns a deep amber color, about 5-7 minutes. Be careful not to let it burn.
    - Remove the pan from heat and carefully add the heavy cream, butter, and vanilla extract. The mixture will bubble up, so be cautious.

- Stir the caramel until smooth and well combined. Let it cool slightly.
5. Assemble the Pie:
    - Spread the chopped toasted walnuts evenly over the bottom of the prepared pie crust.
    - Pour the warm caramel filling over the walnuts, distributing it evenly.
6. Bake the Pie:
    - Place the pie in the preheated oven and bake for 20-25 minutes, or until the crust is golden brown and the filling is bubbly.
7. Cool and Serve:
    - Allow the pie to cool completely on a wire rack before serving. The caramel will set as it cools.
8. Enjoy:
    - Slice and serve the caramel walnut pie at room temperature. Optionally, you can serve it with a dollop of whipped cream or a scoop of vanilla ice cream.

Tips:

- To toast the walnuts, spread them in a single layer on a baking sheet and toast in a preheated oven at 350°F (175°C) for about 8-10 minutes, stirring halfway through, until fragrant.
- Handle the caramel carefully as it can be very hot. Work with caution to avoid burns.
- Store any leftover pie in the refrigerator, covered with plastic wrap or in an airtight container, for up to 3-4 days.

Walnut and Kale Pesto

Ingredients:

- 2 cups packed kale leaves, stems removed
- 1/2 cup walnuts, toasted
- 1/2 cup grated Parmesan cheese
- 2 cloves garlic, peeled
- 1/2 cup extra virgin olive oil
- 1 tablespoon fresh lemon juice
- Salt and pepper, to taste

Instructions:

1. Prepare the Kale and Walnuts:
    - If not already toasted, toast the walnuts in a dry skillet over medium heat for about 5 minutes, stirring frequently, until fragrant. Let them cool.
    - Blanch the kale leaves in boiling water for about 1-2 minutes until bright green and slightly tender. Drain and rinse under cold water to stop the cooking process. Squeeze out excess water.
2. Blend the Pesto:
    - In a food processor, combine the blanched kale leaves, toasted walnuts, grated Parmesan cheese, and peeled garlic cloves.
    - Pulse several times until the mixture is finely chopped.
3. Add Olive Oil and Lemon Juice:
    - With the food processor running, slowly drizzle in the extra virgin olive oil and fresh lemon juice. Continue blending until the pesto reaches your desired consistency. You may need to stop and scrape down the sides of the bowl with a spatula.
4. Season to Taste:
    - Add salt and pepper to taste. Remember that Parmesan cheese adds saltiness, so adjust accordingly.
5. Serve or Store:
    - Transfer the walnut and kale pesto to a bowl or jar. It can be used immediately or stored in the refrigerator for up to 1 week.

Tips:

- Variations: For added depth of flavor, you can incorporate a handful of fresh basil leaves or parsley into the pesto mixture.
- Uses: This pesto is versatile and can be used as a pasta sauce, spread on sandwiches, stirred into soups, or as a topping for grilled meats and vegetables.
- Storage: To store pesto for longer periods, you can freeze it in ice cube trays and then transfer the frozen cubes to a freezer bag. This allows you to thaw only what you need later on.

This walnut and kale pesto is not only delicious but also packed with nutrients, making it a great addition to your culinary repertoire!

Walnut Encrusted Pork Chops

Ingredients:

- 4 boneless pork chops, about 1 inch thick
- 1 cup walnuts, finely chopped
- 1/2 cup panko breadcrumbs
- 1/4 cup grated Parmesan cheese
- 1 teaspoon dried thyme
- 1/2 teaspoon garlic powder
- Salt and pepper, to taste
- 2 eggs, beaten
- 2 tablespoons Dijon mustard
- 2 tablespoons olive oil, for cooking

Instructions:

1. Preheat the Oven:
    - Preheat your oven to 375°F (190°C). Prepare a baking sheet by lining it with parchment paper or greasing it lightly with olive oil.
2. Prepare the Pork Chops:
    - Pat dry the pork chops with paper towels and season both sides with salt and pepper.
3. Prepare the Walnut Coating:
    - In a shallow dish or bowl, combine the finely chopped walnuts, panko breadcrumbs, grated Parmesan cheese, dried thyme, garlic powder, and a pinch of salt and pepper. Mix well.
4. Coat the Pork Chops:
    - In another shallow dish or bowl, whisk together the beaten eggs and Dijon mustard.
    - Dip each pork chop into the egg and mustard mixture, coating both sides evenly.
    - Then, press each pork chop into the walnut mixture, ensuring the chops are thoroughly coated on all sides with the walnut crust.
5. Cook the Pork Chops:
    - Heat olive oil in a large oven-safe skillet over medium-high heat.
    - Once the oil is hot, add the pork chops to the skillet (you may need to do this in batches depending on the size of your skillet). Cook for 2-3 minutes on each side, until the walnut crust is golden brown and crispy.
6. Finish in the Oven:
    - Transfer the skillet with the seared pork chops to the preheated oven.
    - Bake for 10-15 minutes, or until the internal temperature of the pork chops reaches 145°F (63°C) for medium-rare to medium doneness. Cooking time may vary depending on the thickness of your pork chops.
7. Serve:

- - Remove the walnut encrusted pork chops from the oven and let them rest for a few minutes before serving.
  - Serve hot, garnished with fresh herbs if desired. These pork chops pair well with roasted vegetables, mashed potatoes, or a crisp salad.

Tips:

- Ensure your skillet is oven-safe to avoid transferring the pork chops to a different baking dish before baking.
- Adjust the cooking time based on the thickness of your pork chops to ensure they are cooked through but still juicy.
- Feel free to customize the seasoning in the walnut coating with herbs and spices of your choice for added flavor.

Walnut Bread

Ingredients:

- 2 cups all-purpose flour
- 1 cup whole wheat flour
- 1/2 cup rolled oats
- 1/2 cup chopped walnuts, toasted
- 1 tablespoon sugar
- 2 teaspoons baking powder
- 1 teaspoon baking soda
- 1 teaspoon salt
- 1 1/2 cups buttermilk (or substitute with milk mixed with 1 tablespoon of vinegar or lemon juice)
- 1/4 cup unsalted butter, melted
- 1 large egg
- 1/4 cup honey (optional, for added sweetness)

Instructions:

1. Preheat the Oven:
    - Preheat your oven to 350°F (175°C). Grease a 9x5-inch loaf pan or line it with parchment paper.
2. Prepare the Walnuts:
    - Spread the chopped walnuts on a baking sheet and toast them in the preheated oven for about 5-7 minutes, until lightly golden and fragrant. Remove and let them cool.
3. Mix Dry Ingredients:
    - In a large bowl, whisk together the all-purpose flour, whole wheat flour, rolled oats, sugar, baking powder, baking soda, and salt.
4. Combine Wet Ingredients:
    - In another bowl, whisk together the buttermilk, melted butter, egg, and honey (if using).
5. Combine Wet and Dry Ingredients:
    - Pour the wet ingredients into the bowl of dry ingredients. Stir gently with a wooden spoon or spatula until just combined. Do not overmix.
6. Fold in Walnuts:
    - Gently fold in the toasted chopped walnuts until evenly distributed throughout the batter.
7. Bake the Bread:
    - Pour the batter into the prepared loaf pan, spreading it out evenly.
    - Bake in the preheated oven for 45-55 minutes, or until a toothpick inserted into the center comes out clean.
8. Cool and Serve:

- Remove the walnut bread from the oven and let it cool in the pan for 10 minutes. Then, transfer it to a wire rack to cool completely before slicing.
9. Enjoy:
    - Slice and serve the walnut bread plain, toasted with butter, or with your favorite spread.

Tips:

- To keep the walnuts crunchy, make sure they are completely cooled before adding them to the batter.
- If you prefer a sweeter bread, you can increase the amount of sugar or honey.
- Store leftover walnut bread in an airtight container at room temperature for up to 3 days. You can also freeze slices wrapped in plastic wrap and stored in a freezer bag for longer storage.

This Walnut Bread is perfect for breakfast, snacking, or as a side to soups and salads. Enjoy its nutty flavor and wholesome texture!

Chocolate Walnut Fudge

Ingredients:

- 2 cups semi-sweet chocolate chips
- 1 (14 oz) can sweetened condensed milk
- 1 teaspoon vanilla extract
- 1/4 teaspoon salt
- 1 cup chopped walnuts (toasted, if desired)
- Optional: Extra chopped walnuts for topping

Instructions:

1. Prepare the Pan:
    - Line an 8x8 inch baking pan with parchment paper or aluminum foil, leaving some overhang for easy removal later. Grease lightly with butter or cooking spray.
2. Melt Chocolate:
    - In a medium saucepan, combine the chocolate chips and sweetened condensed milk over low heat. Stir constantly until the chocolate is melted and the mixture is smooth.
3. Add Flavorings:
    - Remove the saucepan from heat. Stir in the vanilla extract and salt until well combined.
4. Mix in Walnuts:
    - Fold in the chopped walnuts until evenly distributed throughout the fudge mixture.
5. Pour into Pan:
    - Pour the fudge mixture into the prepared baking pan. Use a spatula to smooth the top and spread it evenly.
6. Optional Topping:
    - Sprinkle additional chopped walnuts on top of the fudge and gently press them into the surface.
7. Chill:
    - Refrigerate the fudge for at least 2 hours, or until firm.
8. Cut and Serve:
    - Once the fudge is completely set, lift it out of the pan using the overhang of parchment paper or foil. Place it on a cutting board and cut into small squares using a sharp knife.
9. Enjoy:
    - Serve the chocolate walnut fudge at room temperature and enjoy its rich, creamy texture with the added crunch of walnuts.

Tips:

- For extra flavor, you can toast the walnuts before chopping them. Simply spread them on a baking sheet and toast in a preheated oven at 350°F (175°C) for about 5-7 minutes, stirring occasionally, until fragrant.
- Store the chocolate walnut fudge in an airtight container at room temperature for up to 1 week. You can also store it in the refrigerator for longer shelf life.
- Feel free to customize the recipe by adding other mix-ins such as dried fruit, marshmallows, or a swirl of peanut butter before chilling.

This Chocolate Walnut Fudge makes a wonderful treat for holidays, parties, or any time you crave something sweet and indulgent!

Walnut and Pear Salad

Ingredients:

- 4 cups mixed salad greens (such as arugula, spinach, and/or spring mix)
- 2 ripe pears, cored and thinly sliced
- 1/2 cup walnuts, toasted and chopped
- 1/4 cup crumbled blue cheese or goat cheese (optional)
- 1/4 cup dried cranberries or cherries (optional)
- 1/4 cup red onion, thinly sliced (optional)
- Freshly ground black pepper, to taste

For the Vinaigrette:

- 1/4 cup extra virgin olive oil
- 2 tablespoons balsamic vinegar
- 1 tablespoon honey or maple syrup
- 1 teaspoon Dijon mustard
- Salt, to taste

Instructions:

1. Prepare the Vinaigrette:
   - In a small bowl or jar, whisk together the extra virgin olive oil, balsamic vinegar, honey or maple syrup, Dijon mustard, and a pinch of salt until well combined. Set aside.
2. Assemble the Salad:
   - In a large salad bowl, combine the mixed salad greens, thinly sliced pears, toasted and chopped walnuts, crumbled blue cheese or goat cheese (if using), dried cranberries or cherries (if using), and thinly sliced red onion (if using).
3. Drizzle with Vinaigrette:
   - Drizzle the prepared vinaigrette over the salad ingredients. Start with a portion of the dressing and toss gently to coat everything evenly. Add more dressing as needed, to taste.
4. Season with Black Pepper:
   - Season the salad with freshly ground black pepper, to taste.
5. Serve:
   - Serve the walnut and pear salad immediately as a side dish or add grilled chicken or shrimp to make it a complete meal.

Tips:

- Toasting Walnuts: To toast walnuts, spread them in a single layer on a baking sheet and toast in a preheated oven at 350°F (175°C) for about 5-7 minutes, stirring halfway through, until fragrant and lightly golden.

- Variations: Feel free to customize the salad by adding other ingredients like avocado slices, roasted beets, or a different type of cheese such as feta or Parmesan.
- Make-Ahead: You can prepare the vinaigrette ahead of time and store it in the refrigerator. Toss the salad ingredients with the dressing just before serving to keep the greens crisp.

This Walnut and Pear Salad is not only delicious but also a perfect balance of flavors and textures. Enjoy it for a light lunch or as a refreshing side dish!

Walnut and Cranberry Granola

Ingredients:

- 3 cups old-fashioned rolled oats
- 1 cup walnuts, chopped
- 1/2 cup honey or maple syrup
- 1/4 cup coconut oil, melted
- 1 teaspoon vanilla extract
- 1/2 teaspoon ground cinnamon
- 1/2 teaspoon salt
- 1 cup dried cranberries
- Optional: 1/2 cup unsweetened shredded coconut

Instructions:

1. Preheat the Oven:
    - Preheat your oven to 300°F (150°C). Line a large baking sheet with parchment paper or a silicone baking mat.
2. Mix Dry Ingredients:
    - In a large bowl, combine the rolled oats and chopped walnuts. If using, add the unsweetened shredded coconut as well.
3. Prepare the Wet Ingredients:
    - In a small bowl, whisk together the honey or maple syrup, melted coconut oil, vanilla extract, ground cinnamon, and salt until well combined.
4. Combine Dry and Wet Ingredients:
    - Pour the wet mixture over the dry oat and walnut mixture. Stir well until all the oats and nuts are evenly coated with the liquid mixture.
5. Spread on Baking Sheet:
    - Spread the granola mixture evenly onto the prepared baking sheet in a single layer. Press it down slightly with the back of a spoon or spatula to compact it.
6. Bake the Granola:
    - Bake in the preheated oven for 30-35 minutes, stirring halfway through, until the granola is golden brown and crisp.
7. Add Cranberries:
    - Remove the baking sheet from the oven and sprinkle the dried cranberries evenly over the hot granola. Press them gently into the granola.
8. Cool Completely:
    - Allow the granola to cool completely on the baking sheet. It will continue to crisp up as it cools.
9. Store:
    - Once completely cooled, transfer the walnut and cranberry granola to an airtight container or glass jar for storage.

Tips:

- Customize: Feel free to customize this granola recipe by adding other dried fruits like raisins or apricots, or incorporating seeds such as pumpkin seeds or sunflower seeds.
- Serve: Enjoy this granola with yogurt, milk, or as a topping for smoothie bowls.
- Storage: Store the granola in a cool, dry place for up to 2 weeks or in the refrigerator for longer shelf life.

This Walnut and Cranberry Granola is not only delicious but also packed with wholesome ingredients to fuel your day!

Spiced Walnut Loaf

Ingredients:

- 1 1/2 cups all-purpose flour
- 1 teaspoon baking powder
- 1/2 teaspoon baking soda
- 1/2 teaspoon salt
- 1 teaspoon ground cinnamon
- 1/2 teaspoon ground ginger
- 1/4 teaspoon ground nutmeg
- 1/4 teaspoon ground cloves
- 1/2 cup unsalted butter, softened
- 1/2 cup granulated sugar
- 1/2 cup brown sugar, packed
- 2 large eggs
- 1 teaspoon vanilla extract
- 1/2 cup buttermilk (or substitute with milk mixed with 1/2 tablespoon of vinegar or lemon juice)
- 1 cup chopped walnuts, toasted
- Optional: Powdered sugar, for dusting

Instructions:

1. Preheat the Oven:
    - Preheat your oven to 350°F (175°C). Grease and flour a 9x5-inch loaf pan, or line it with parchment paper for easy removal.
2. Toast the Walnuts:
    - Spread the chopped walnuts on a baking sheet and toast them in the preheated oven for about 5-7 minutes, until fragrant. Let them cool while you prepare the batter.
3. Prepare Dry Ingredients:
    - In a medium bowl, whisk together the all-purpose flour, baking powder, baking soda, salt, ground cinnamon, ground ginger, ground nutmeg, and ground cloves. Set aside.
4. Cream Butter and Sugars:
    - In a large bowl, using an electric mixer or stand mixer fitted with the paddle attachment, cream together the softened butter, granulated sugar, and brown sugar until light and fluffy.
5. Add Eggs and Vanilla:
    - Add the eggs one at a time, beating well after each addition. Stir in the vanilla extract.
6. Alternate Adding Dry Ingredients and Buttermilk:

- Gradually add the flour mixture to the butter-sugar mixture in three additions, alternating with the buttermilk. Begin and end with the flour mixture. Mix until just combined after each addition, being careful not to overmix.
7. Fold in Walnuts:
    - Gently fold in the toasted chopped walnuts until evenly distributed in the batter.
8. Bake the Loaf:
    - Pour the batter into the prepared loaf pan and spread it out evenly.
    - Bake in the preheated oven for 50-60 minutes, or until a toothpick inserted into the center comes out clean or with a few moist crumbs.
9. Cool and Serve:
    - Allow the spiced walnut loaf to cool in the pan for 10 minutes before transferring it to a wire rack to cool completely.
10. Optional Dusting:
    - Once cooled, dust the top of the loaf with powdered sugar for a decorative finish.
11. Slice and Enjoy:
    - Slice the spiced walnut loaf and serve it plain, toasted with butter, or with a dollop of whipped cream or ice cream.

Tips:

- Storage: Store the cooled spiced walnut loaf in an airtight container at room temperature for up to 3-4 days.
- Variations: Feel free to customize the spices to your liking or add dried fruits such as raisins or chopped dates for extra flavor and texture.
- Freezing: This loaf freezes well. Wrap it tightly in plastic wrap and aluminum foil before freezing for up to 2-3 months.

This Spiced Walnut Loaf is perfect for enjoying with a cup of tea or coffee, and its warm spices and nutty flavor make it a wonderful treat during cooler months.

Walnut Chicken Salad

Ingredients:

- 2 cups cooked chicken breast, shredded or diced (about 2 medium chicken breasts)
- 1/2 cup chopped walnuts, toasted
- 1/2 cup celery, diced
- 1/4 cup red onion, finely chopped
- 1/4 cup dried cranberries or grapes, halved (optional, for sweetness)
- 1/2 cup mayonnaise
- 2 tablespoons plain Greek yogurt (or sour cream)
- 1 tablespoon Dijon mustard
- 1 tablespoon lemon juice
- Salt and pepper, to taste
- Fresh parsley or chives, chopped (optional, for garnish)
- Lettuce leaves or sandwich bread, for serving

Instructions:

1. Prepare the Chicken:
    - Cook the chicken breasts by boiling, baking, or grilling them until fully cooked. Let them cool, then shred or dice them into bite-sized pieces.
2. Toast the Walnuts:
    - Spread the chopped walnuts on a baking sheet and toast in a preheated oven at 350°F (175°C) for about 5-7 minutes, stirring occasionally, until fragrant and lightly golden. Remove from the oven and let them cool.
3. Prepare the Salad:
    - In a large mixing bowl, combine the cooked chicken, toasted walnuts, diced celery, chopped red onion, and dried cranberries or grapes (if using).
4. Make the Dressing:
    - In a small bowl, whisk together the mayonnaise, Greek yogurt (or sour cream), Dijon mustard, and lemon juice until smooth and well combined.
5. Combine and Season:
    - Pour the dressing over the chicken mixture. Gently toss until all ingredients are evenly coated with the dressing. Season with salt and pepper to taste.
6. Chill (Optional):
    - For best flavor, cover the chicken salad and refrigerate for at least 30 minutes to allow the flavors to meld together.
7. Serve:
    - Serve the walnut chicken salad on a bed of lettuce leaves as a salad, or as a sandwich filling between slices of bread or in a wrap.
8. Garnish (Optional):
    - Garnish with chopped fresh parsley or chives before serving, if desired.

Tips:

- Variations: Feel free to add additional ingredients such as diced apples, grapes, or avocado for added sweetness and creaminess.
- Storage: Store leftover chicken salad in an airtight container in the refrigerator for up to 3-4 days.
- Meal Prep: This salad is great for meal prepping lunches or quick dinners during busy weekdays.

This Walnut Chicken Salad is versatile, satisfying, and perfect for a light and flavorful meal. Enjoy it chilled on its own or as a filling for sandwiches and wraps!

Walnut Coffee Cake

Ingredients:

For the Cake:

- 1/2 cup unsalted butter, softened
- 1 cup granulated sugar
- 2 large eggs
- 1 teaspoon vanilla extract
- 1 cup sour cream or Greek yogurt
- 2 cups all-purpose flour
- 1 teaspoon baking powder
- 1 teaspoon baking soda
- 1/2 teaspoon salt

For the Walnut Streusel:

- 1/2 cup packed brown sugar
- 1/2 cup all-purpose flour
- 1 teaspoon ground cinnamon
- 1/4 cup cold unsalted butter, cut into small pieces
- 1 cup chopped walnuts

Instructions:

1. Preheat the Oven:
    - Preheat your oven to 350°F (175°C). Grease and flour a 9x9-inch baking pan or line it with parchment paper for easy removal.
2. Make the Walnut Streusel:
    - In a medium bowl, combine the brown sugar, flour, and ground cinnamon for the streusel topping.
    - Cut in the cold butter using a pastry cutter or your fingers until the mixture resembles coarse crumbs. Stir in the chopped walnuts. Set aside.
3. Prepare the Cake Batter:
    - In a large mixing bowl, cream together the softened butter and granulated sugar until light and fluffy.
    - Beat in the eggs, one at a time, until well combined. Stir in the vanilla extract and sour cream (or Greek yogurt) until smooth.
4. Combine Dry Ingredients:
    - In a separate bowl, whisk together the flour, baking powder, baking soda, and salt.
5. Combine Wet and Dry Ingredients:
    - Gradually add the dry ingredients to the wet ingredients, mixing until just combined. Do not overmix.

6. Assemble the Coffee Cake:
    - Spread half of the cake batter into the prepared baking pan, smoothing it out evenly with a spatula.
    - Sprinkle half of the walnut streusel mixture over the batter in the pan.
    - Carefully spread the remaining cake batter over the streusel layer, smoothing it out gently.
    - Top evenly with the remaining walnut streusel mixture.
7. Bake the Coffee Cake:
    - Bake in the preheated oven for 35-40 minutes, or until a toothpick inserted into the center comes out clean and the top is golden brown.
8. Cool and Serve:
    - Allow the walnut coffee cake to cool in the pan for 10-15 minutes before transferring it to a wire rack to cool completely.
9. Optional Glaze (if desired):
    - For added sweetness, you can drizzle the cooled coffee cake with a simple glaze made from powdered sugar and a little milk or water.
10. Slice and Enjoy:
    - Slice the walnut coffee cake into squares and serve warm or at room temperature. Enjoy with a cup of coffee or tea!

Tips:

- Storage: Store leftover walnut coffee cake in an airtight container at room temperature for up to 3 days. It can also be stored in the refrigerator for longer shelf life.
- Variations: Feel free to add a pinch of nutmeg or cardamom to the streusel for additional flavor.
- Serve: This coffee cake is perfect for breakfast, brunch, or as a delightful dessert for any occasion.

This Walnut Coffee Cake recipe is sure to become a favorite with its tender crumb, crunchy walnut streusel topping, and delicious flavor profile!

Walnut and Goat Cheese Crostini

Ingredients:

- 1 French baguette, sliced into 1/2-inch thick rounds
- 4 oz goat cheese, softened
- 1/2 cup chopped walnuts, toasted
- Honey, for drizzling
- Fresh thyme leaves, for garnish
- Olive oil, for brushing
- Salt and pepper, to taste

Instructions:

1. Prepare the Baguette:
    - Preheat your oven to 375°F (190°C). Arrange the baguette slices on a baking sheet in a single layer.
2. Toast the Baguette:
    - Lightly brush olive oil on both sides of each baguette slice. Sprinkle lightly with salt and pepper.
    - Bake in the preheated oven for about 8-10 minutes, or until the bread slices are crisp and lightly golden. Remove from the oven and let them cool slightly.
3. Prepare the Goat Cheese Mixture:
    - In a small bowl, mix the softened goat cheese until smooth and creamy.
4. Assemble the Crostini:
    - Spread a generous amount of goat cheese onto each toasted baguette slice.
    - Sprinkle chopped toasted walnuts evenly over the goat cheese layer.
5. Drizzle with Honey:
    - Drizzle honey over each crostini. The amount can vary based on your preference for sweetness.
6. Garnish:
    - Garnish each crostini with fresh thyme leaves for a pop of color and added flavor.
7. Serve:
    - Arrange the walnut and goat cheese crostini on a platter and serve immediately as a delicious appetizer or snack.

Tips:

- Toasting Walnuts: Spread chopped walnuts on a baking sheet and toast in a preheated oven at 350°F (175°C) for about 5-7 minutes, stirring occasionally, until fragrant and lightly golden.
- Variations: Add a thin slice of fresh pear or fig on top of each crostini before drizzling with honey for an extra layer of flavor and texture.

- Make-Ahead: You can prepare the toasted baguette slices and goat cheese mixture in advance. Assemble the crostini just before serving to keep the bread crispy.

These Walnut and Goat Cheese Crostini are sure to impress with their combination of flavors and textures, making them perfect for entertaining or enjoying as a savory snack!

Walnut Pate

Ingredients:

- 1 cup walnuts, toasted
- 1/4 cup olive oil
- 1 small onion, finely chopped
- 2 cloves garlic, minced
- 1 tablespoon fresh thyme leaves (or 1 teaspoon dried thyme)
- 1/4 cup fresh parsley, chopped
- 1 tablespoon lemon juice
- Salt and pepper, to taste

Instructions:

1. Toast the Walnuts:
    - Spread the walnuts on a baking sheet and toast them in a preheated oven at 350°F (175°C) for about 5-7 minutes, stirring occasionally, until fragrant. Let them cool.
2. Prepare the Pâté:
    - In a skillet, heat the olive oil over medium heat. Add the chopped onion and sauté until softened and translucent, about 5-7 minutes.
    - Add the minced garlic and thyme to the skillet, and cook for an additional 1-2 minutes until fragrant.
3. Blend the Ingredients:
    - In a food processor, combine the toasted walnuts, sautéed onion mixture, chopped parsley, and lemon juice.
    - Pulse the mixture until smooth and well combined. Scrape down the sides of the food processor as needed and continue blending until you reach a smooth consistency.
4. Season to Taste:
    - Season the walnut pâté with salt and pepper to taste. Adjust the seasoning as needed.
5. Chill (Optional):
    - For best flavor, transfer the walnut pâté to a serving dish or container, cover, and refrigerate for at least 1 hour to allow the flavors to meld together.
6. Serve:
    - Serve the walnut pâté at room temperature or chilled, spread on toasted bread, crackers, or as a dip for vegetable sticks.

Tips:

- Variations: You can customize this walnut pâté by adding a dash of cayenne pepper for a spicy kick, or a tablespoon of balsamic vinegar for added depth of flavor.

- Storage: Store any leftover walnut pâté in an airtight container in the refrigerator for up to 5 days. Bring to room temperature before serving.
- Presentation: Garnish the walnut pâté with additional fresh herbs, a drizzle of olive oil, or a sprinkle of chopped walnuts before serving for an elegant touch.

This Walnut Pâté is not only flavorful and versatile but also easy to make, making it a great addition to your appetizer repertoire for gatherings or everyday snacking. Enjoy its rich, nutty taste spread on your favorite bread or crackers!

Walnut and Roasted Red Pepper Spread

Ingredients:

- 1 cup walnuts, toasted
- 1 cup roasted red peppers (from a jar or homemade), drained and chopped
- 2 cloves garlic, minced
- 2 tablespoons olive oil
- 1 tablespoon lemon juice
- 1 tablespoon tomato paste
- 1/2 teaspoon smoked paprika
- Salt and pepper, to taste
- Fresh parsley or basil, chopped (optional, for garnish)

Instructions:

1. Toast the Walnuts:
   - Spread the walnuts on a baking sheet and toast them in a preheated oven at 350°F (175°C) for about 5-7 minutes, stirring occasionally, until fragrant. Let them cool.
2. Prepare the Spread:
   - In a food processor or blender, combine the toasted walnuts, chopped roasted red peppers, minced garlic, olive oil, lemon juice, tomato paste, and smoked paprika.
3. Blend Until Smooth:
   - Pulse or blend the mixture until smooth and well combined. Scrape down the sides of the food processor or blender as needed to ensure everything is evenly mixed.
4. Season to Taste:
   - Season the spread with salt and pepper to taste. Adjust the seasoning as needed, adding more lemon juice or olive oil if desired for consistency.
5. Chill (Optional):
   - Transfer the walnut and roasted red pepper spread to a serving bowl or container. Cover and refrigerate for at least 30 minutes to allow the flavors to meld together.
6. Serve:
   - Garnish the spread with chopped fresh parsley or basil, if desired. Serve at room temperature or chilled, spread on bread or crackers, or as a dip for vegetables.

Tips:

- Roasting Red Peppers: If you prefer to roast your own red peppers, you can do so by placing them under a broiler or directly over a gas flame until the skin is charred. Let them cool in a covered bowl, then peel off the skin and remove the seeds before using.

- Storage: Store any leftover walnut and roasted red pepper spread in an airtight container in the refrigerator for up to 5 days.
- Variations: For a spicier version, add a pinch of crushed red pepper flakes or a dash of hot sauce. You can also experiment with adding herbs like basil or oregano for added freshness.

This Walnut and Roasted Red Pepper Spread is versatile and full of flavor, making it a great addition to your appetizer menu or as a quick and tasty snack. Enjoy its creamy texture and delicious taste!

Chocolate Walnut Biscotti

Ingredients:

- 2 cups all-purpose flour
- 1/2 cup unsweetened cocoa powder
- 1 teaspoon baking powder
- 1/2 teaspoon baking soda
- 1/2 teaspoon salt
- 1/2 cup unsalted butter, softened
- 1 cup granulated sugar
- 2 large eggs
- 1 teaspoon vanilla extract
- 1 cup walnuts, chopped
- 1 cup semisweet chocolate chips or chunks

Instructions:

1. Preheat Oven and Prepare Baking Sheet:
    - Preheat your oven to 350°F (175°C). Line a baking sheet with parchment paper or a silicone baking mat.
2. Mix Dry Ingredients:
    - In a medium bowl, whisk together the flour, cocoa powder, baking powder, baking soda, and salt until well combined. Set aside.
3. Cream Butter and Sugar:
    - In a large bowl or the bowl of a stand mixer, cream together the softened butter and granulated sugar until light and fluffy.
4. Add Eggs and Vanilla:
    - Add the eggs one at a time, beating well after each addition. Stir in the vanilla extract.
5. Combine Wet and Dry Ingredients:
    - Gradually add the dry ingredients to the butter mixture, mixing until just combined. The dough will be stiff.
6. Fold in Walnuts and Chocolate:
    - Gently fold in the chopped walnuts and semisweet chocolate chips or chunks until evenly distributed throughout the dough.
7. Shape the Dough:
    - Divide the dough in half. On the prepared baking sheet, shape each half into a log about 12 inches long and 2 inches wide, spacing them a few inches apart.
8. Bake the Biscotti Logs:
    - Bake in the preheated oven for 25-30 minutes, or until the logs are firm to the touch and slightly cracked on top.
9. Cool Slightly:

- Remove the baking sheet from the oven and let the biscotti logs cool on the pan for 10-15 minutes. Reduce the oven temperature to 325°F (160°C) during this time.
10. **Slice the Biscotti:**
    - Using a sharp serrated knife, slice the logs diagonally into 1/2-inch thick slices.
11. **Bake Again:**
    - Arrange the biscotti slices cut side down on the baking sheet. Bake for an additional 10-12 minutes, flipping them halfway through, until the biscotti are crisp and dry.
12. **Cool Completely:**
    - Remove the biscotti from the oven and transfer them to a wire rack to cool completely. They will continue to crisp up as they cool.
13. **Optional Drizzle (if desired):**
    - Melt additional chocolate chips or chunks and drizzle over the cooled biscotti for decoration.
14. **Serve and Store:**
    - Once completely cooled and any optional drizzle has set, store the biscotti in an airtight container at room temperature for up to 2 weeks.

Tips:

- Toasting Walnuts: For extra flavor, toast the walnuts before chopping and adding them to the dough. Spread them on a baking sheet and toast in a preheated oven at 350°F (175°C) for about 5-7 minutes, stirring occasionally, until fragrant.
- Variations: For a different twist, you can add a teaspoon of orange zest or espresso powder to the dough for added flavor complexity.
- Serve Suggestions: Enjoy these chocolate walnut biscotti with a cup of coffee or tea, or package them in a decorative tin for a lovely homemade gift.

These Chocolate Walnut Biscotti are perfect for any occasion, whether it's a special treat for yourself or to share with friends and family. Enjoy their rich chocolate flavor and satisfying crunch!

Walnut and Quinoa Stuffed Peppers

Ingredients:

- 4 large bell peppers (any color), tops cut off and seeds removed
- 1 cup quinoa, rinsed
- 2 cups vegetable broth or water
- 1 tablespoon olive oil
- 1 small onion, finely chopped
- 2 cloves garlic, minced
- 1/2 cup walnuts, chopped
- 1 teaspoon ground cumin
- 1 teaspoon smoked paprika
- 1/2 teaspoon dried oregano
- Salt and pepper, to taste
- 1 (15-ounce) can black beans, drained and rinsed
- 1 cup corn kernels (fresh or frozen)
- 1/2 cup diced tomatoes (canned or fresh)
- 1/4 cup fresh cilantro or parsley, chopped
- 1/2 cup shredded cheese (cheddar, mozzarella, or vegan cheese), optional

Instructions:

1. Preheat Oven:
   - Preheat your oven to 375°F (190°C). Prepare a baking dish that can hold the stuffed peppers upright.
2. Prepare Quinoa:
   - In a medium saucepan, bring the vegetable broth or water to a boil. Add the rinsed quinoa, reduce heat to low, cover, and simmer for about 15-20 minutes, or until the quinoa is cooked and fluffy. Remove from heat and fluff with a fork.
3. Prepare Bell Peppers:
   - While the quinoa is cooking, prepare the bell peppers by cutting off the tops and removing the seeds and membranes. If needed, trim the bottoms slightly so they can stand upright in the baking dish.
4. Sauté Onion and Garlic:
   - In a large skillet, heat olive oil over medium heat. Add the chopped onion and sauté until softened, about 5-7 minutes. Add the minced garlic and cook for another 1-2 minutes until fragrant.
5. Toast Walnuts and Add Spices:
   - Add the chopped walnuts to the skillet with the onions and garlic. Toast them for 2-3 minutes until lightly golden and fragrant.
   - Stir in the ground cumin, smoked paprika, dried oregano, salt, and pepper. Cook for another minute until the spices are aromatic.
6. Combine Quinoa Mixture:

- Add the cooked quinoa, black beans, corn kernels, diced tomatoes, and chopped cilantro or parsley to the skillet. Stir well to combine all the ingredients. Taste and adjust seasoning if needed.
7. Stuff the Peppers:
    - Stuff each bell pepper with the quinoa mixture, pressing down gently to pack it in. Depending on the size of your peppers, you may have some filling leftover.
8. Bake the Stuffed Peppers:
    - Place the stuffed peppers upright in the prepared baking dish. If desired, sprinkle shredded cheese on top of each stuffed pepper.
    - Cover the baking dish with foil and bake in the preheated oven for 30-35 minutes, or until the peppers are tender and the filling is heated through.
9. Serve:
    - Remove the foil and garnish the stuffed peppers with additional chopped cilantro or parsley before serving. Enjoy hot as a main dish.

Tips:

- Variations: Feel free to customize the filling by adding other vegetables such as spinach, zucchini, or mushrooms. You can also use different types of cheese or omit it for a vegan option.
- Make-Ahead: Prepare the quinoa mixture and stuff the peppers up to a day in advance. Keep them covered in the refrigerator until ready to bake.
- Leftovers: Stuffed peppers make great leftovers. Store them in an airtight container in the refrigerator for up to 3 days.

These Walnut and Quinoa Stuffed Peppers are not only delicious and satisfying but also packed with protein and nutrients. They make a wholesome meal that's sure to please everyone at the table!

Walnut and Spinach Stuffed Chicken

Ingredients:

- 4 boneless, skinless chicken breasts
- Salt and pepper, to taste
- 1 tablespoon olive oil

For the Filling:

- 2 cups fresh spinach leaves, chopped
- 1/2 cup chopped walnuts
- 1/2 cup ricotta cheese
- 1/4 cup grated Parmesan cheese
- 2 cloves garlic, minced
- 1 tablespoon fresh basil, chopped (or 1 teaspoon dried basil)
- Salt and pepper, to taste

For the Sauce (optional):

- 1 tablespoon butter
- 1 tablespoon all-purpose flour
- 1 cup chicken broth
- 1/4 cup heavy cream
- Salt and pepper, to taste

Instructions:

1. Preheat Oven:
   - Preheat your oven to 375°F (190°C).
2. Prepare Chicken Breasts:
   - Place each chicken breast between two pieces of plastic wrap. Using a meat mallet or rolling pin, pound them to an even thickness of about 1/4 to 1/2 inch. Season both sides with salt and pepper.
3. Make the Filling:
   - In a medium bowl, combine chopped spinach, chopped walnuts, ricotta cheese, Parmesan cheese, minced garlic, chopped basil, salt, and pepper. Mix until well combined.
4. Stuff the Chicken:
   - Spoon the spinach and walnut mixture evenly onto each chicken breast, leaving about 1/2 inch border around the edges. Roll up each chicken breast and secure with toothpicks or kitchen twine to keep the filling inside.
5. Sear the Chicken:
   - Heat olive oil in an oven-proof skillet over medium-high heat. Add the stuffed chicken breasts and cook for about 2-3 minutes per side, or until browned.
6. Bake the Chicken:

- Transfer the skillet to the preheated oven. Bake for 20-25 minutes, or until the chicken is cooked through (internal temperature should reach 165°F or 75°C).
7. **Make the Sauce (optional):**
   - While the chicken is baking, prepare the sauce if desired. In a small saucepan, melt butter over medium heat. Whisk in flour and cook for 1 minute.
   - Gradually whisk in chicken broth and bring to a simmer. Cook until slightly thickened, about 3-5 minutes.
   - Stir in heavy cream and season with salt and pepper to taste. Cook for another 1-2 minutes until heated through.
8. **Serve:**
   - Remove the stuffed chicken breasts from the oven and let them rest for a few minutes. Remove toothpicks or twine before serving.
   - Serve the stuffed chicken breasts drizzled with the optional sauce, if desired. Garnish with additional chopped basil or parsley, if desired.

Tips:

- **Variations:** Feel free to add sun-dried tomatoes, feta cheese, or mushrooms to the filling for additional flavor and texture.
- **Side Dish:** Serve the stuffed chicken with roasted vegetables, mashed potatoes, or a green salad for a complete meal.
- **Make-Ahead:** You can prepare the stuffed chicken breasts up to a day in advance and keep them covered in the refrigerator until ready to bake.

This Walnut and Spinach Stuffed Chicken recipe is elegant enough for a dinner party yet simple enough for a weeknight meal. Enjoy the combination of flavors and textures in every bite!

Walnut Chocolate Chip Cookies

Ingredients:

- 1 cup unsalted butter, softened
- 3/4 cup granulated sugar
- 3/4 cup packed light brown sugar
- 2 large eggs
- 1 teaspoon vanilla extract
- 2 1/4 cups all-purpose flour
- 1 teaspoon baking soda
- 1/2 teaspoon salt
- 1 cup semisweet chocolate chips
- 1 cup chopped walnuts

Instructions:

1. Preheat Oven:
    - Preheat your oven to 375°F (190°C). Line baking sheets with parchment paper or silicone baking mats.
2. Cream Butter and Sugars:
    - In a large bowl or the bowl of a stand mixer, cream together the softened butter, granulated sugar, and brown sugar until light and fluffy.
3. Add Eggs and Vanilla:
    - Beat in the eggs one at a time, then add the vanilla extract. Mix until well combined.
4. Combine Dry Ingredients:
    - In a separate bowl, whisk together the flour, baking soda, and salt.
5. Mix Wet and Dry Ingredients:
    - Gradually add the dry ingredients to the butter mixture, mixing until just combined.
6. Add Chocolate Chips and Walnuts:
    - Stir in the semisweet chocolate chips and chopped walnuts until evenly distributed throughout the dough.
7. Shape Cookies:
    - Drop rounded tablespoons of dough onto the prepared baking sheets, spacing them about 2 inches apart.
8. Bake Cookies:
    - Bake in the preheated oven for 9-11 minutes, or until the edges are golden brown. The centers may still look slightly underdone, which is okay as they will continue to set as they cool.
9. Cool and Serve:
    - Allow the cookies to cool on the baking sheets for 5 minutes before transferring them to wire racks to cool completely.
10. Store:

- Store the walnut chocolate chip cookies in an airtight container at room temperature for up to 1 week. They can also be frozen for longer storage.

Tips:

- Toasting Walnuts: For extra flavor, toast the chopped walnuts in a dry skillet over medium heat for a few minutes until fragrant, stirring frequently.
- Variations: Feel free to use dark chocolate chips or chunks instead of semisweet, or substitute pecans or almonds for the walnuts.
- Soft Cookies: If you prefer softer cookies, slightly underbake them and let them cool completely on the baking sheets before transferring to wire racks.

These Walnut Chocolate Chip Cookies are sure to be a hit with their perfect blend of chewy cookie texture, rich chocolate chips, and crunchy walnuts. Enjoy baking and sharing these delicious treats!

Walnut and Sun-Dried Tomato Pasta

Ingredients:

- 8 ounces (225g) pasta of your choice (such as penne, fusilli, or spaghetti)
- 1/2 cup walnuts, chopped
- 1/2 cup sun-dried tomatoes (packed in oil), drained and chopped
- 2 cloves garlic, minced
- 1/4 cup extra virgin olive oil
- 1/4 teaspoon red pepper flakes (optional, for a bit of heat)
- Salt and freshly ground black pepper, to taste
- Fresh basil or parsley, chopped, for garnish
- Grated Parmesan cheese, for serving (optional)

Instructions:

1. Cook the Pasta:
    - Bring a large pot of salted water to a boil. Cook the pasta according to package instructions until al dente. Reserve about 1/2 cup of pasta cooking water, then drain the pasta.
2. Toast the Walnuts:
    - While the pasta is cooking, toast the chopped walnuts in a dry skillet over medium heat for 3-4 minutes, or until lightly golden and fragrant. Stir frequently to prevent burning. Remove from heat and set aside.
3. Prepare the Sauce:
    - In the same skillet, heat the olive oil over medium heat. Add the minced garlic and cook for about 1 minute, until fragrant.
    - Add the chopped sun-dried tomatoes and red pepper flakes (if using). Cook for another 2-3 minutes, stirring occasionally, to allow the flavors to meld together.
4. Combine Pasta and Sauce:
    - Add the cooked and drained pasta to the skillet with the sun-dried tomatoes and garlic. Toss to coat the pasta evenly with the sauce. If the pasta seems dry, add a bit of the reserved pasta cooking water to loosen it up.
5. Add Walnuts and Season:
    - Stir in the toasted walnuts. Season with salt and freshly ground black pepper to taste. Toss everything together until well combined.
6. Serve:
    - Transfer the Walnut and Sun-Dried Tomato Pasta to serving plates or a large platter. Garnish with chopped fresh basil or parsley.
7. Optional Garnish:
    - If desired, sprinkle grated Parmesan cheese over the pasta just before serving.

Tips:

- Variations: You can add a handful of baby spinach or arugula to the pasta during the last minute of cooking for some added freshness and color.
- Make-Ahead: This pasta dish is best served immediately, but you can prepare the components (toasted walnuts, sun-dried tomato mixture) ahead of time and assemble just before serving.
- Vegetarian/Vegan Options: Omit the Parmesan cheese or use a vegan cheese alternative to make this dish vegan-friendly.

This Walnut and Sun-Dried Tomato Pasta is a flavorful and satisfying dish that's perfect for a quick weeknight dinner or a cozy weekend meal. Enjoy its hearty flavors and textures!

Walnut Blondies

Ingredients:

- 1 cup (2 sticks) unsalted butter, melted
- 1 3/4 cups light brown sugar, packed
- 2 large eggs
- 1 tablespoon vanilla extract
- 2 cups all-purpose flour
- 1/2 teaspoon baking powder
- 1/2 teaspoon salt
- 1 cup walnuts, chopped
- Optional: 1/2 cup chocolate chips or chunks

Instructions:

1. Preheat Oven:
    - Preheat your oven to 350°F (175°C). Grease or line a 9x13-inch baking pan with parchment paper, leaving some overhang for easy removal.
2. Mix Wet Ingredients:
    - In a large bowl, whisk together the melted butter and brown sugar until smooth and well combined.
3. Add Eggs and Vanilla:
    - Add the eggs, one at a time, whisking well after each addition. Stir in the vanilla extract.
4. Combine Dry Ingredients:
    - In a separate bowl, whisk together the flour, baking powder, and salt.
5. Combine Wet and Dry Ingredients:
    - Gradually add the dry ingredients to the wet ingredients, stirring until just combined. Be careful not to overmix.
6. Add Walnuts (and Chocolate Chips, if using):
    - Fold in the chopped walnuts and chocolate chips or chunks, if using, until evenly distributed in the batter.
7. Bake the Blondies:
    - Spread the blondie batter evenly into the prepared baking pan, smoothing the top with a spatula.
    - Bake in the preheated oven for 25-30 minutes, or until the top is golden brown and a toothpick inserted into the center comes out with a few moist crumbs.
8. Cool and Slice:
    - Allow the blondies to cool completely in the pan on a wire rack before slicing into squares.
9. Serve:
    - Once cooled, cut the walnut blondies into squares and serve. Enjoy them as a delicious treat with a glass of milk or a cup of coffee!

Tips:

- Toasting Walnuts: For extra flavor, toast the chopped walnuts in a dry skillet over medium heat for a few minutes until fragrant, stirring frequently. Let them cool before adding to the batter.
- Variations: Feel free to customize these walnut blondies by adding other mix-ins such as butterscotch chips, dried cranberries, or even a swirl of caramel sauce.
- Storage: Store leftover walnut blondies in an airtight container at room temperature for up to 3-4 days, or freeze them for longer storage.

These Walnut Blondies are perfect for any occasion, whether it's a casual snack or a dessert to share with friends and family. Enjoy their buttery richness and the delightful crunch of walnuts in every bite!

Walnut and Pumpkin Bread

Ingredients:

- 1 3/4 cups all-purpose flour
- 1 teaspoon baking soda
- 1/2 teaspoon baking powder
- 1/2 teaspoon salt
- 1 teaspoon ground cinnamon
- 1/2 teaspoon ground nutmeg
- 1/4 teaspoon ground cloves
- 1 cup pumpkin puree (canned or homemade)
- 1/2 cup vegetable oil or melted butter
- 1 cup granulated sugar
- 1/2 cup brown sugar, packed
- 2 large eggs
- 1 teaspoon vanilla extract
- 1/2 cup chopped walnuts
- Optional: 1/2 cup chocolate chips or raisins

Instructions:

1. Preheat Oven and Prepare Pan:
    - Preheat your oven to 350°F (175°C). Grease a 9x5-inch loaf pan with butter or non-stick cooking spray, or line it with parchment paper for easier removal.
2. Mix Dry Ingredients:
    - In a medium bowl, whisk together the flour, baking soda, baking powder, salt, cinnamon, nutmeg, and cloves until well combined. Set aside.
3. Combine Wet Ingredients:
    - In a large bowl, whisk together the pumpkin puree, vegetable oil or melted butter, granulated sugar, brown sugar, eggs, and vanilla extract until smooth and well combined.
4. Combine Wet and Dry Ingredients:
    - Gradually add the dry ingredients to the wet ingredients, stirring with a spatula or wooden spoon until just combined and no streaks of flour remain. Be careful not to overmix.
5. Add Walnuts (and Optional Mix-Ins):
    - Gently fold in the chopped walnuts and any optional mix-ins such as chocolate chips or raisins, if using.
6. Pour Batter into Pan:
    - Pour the batter into the prepared loaf pan and smooth the top with a spatula.
7. Bake the Bread:
    - Bake in the preheated oven for 55-65 minutes, or until a toothpick inserted into the center comes out clean or with a few moist crumbs attached.
8. Cool and Serve:

- Remove the pumpkin bread from the oven and let it cool in the pan for 10 minutes. Then, transfer it to a wire rack to cool completely before slicing.
9. Slice and Enjoy:
    - Once cooled, slice the walnut and pumpkin bread and serve. Enjoy it plain or with a spread of butter or cream cheese.

Tips:

- Pumpkin Puree: Use canned pumpkin puree or homemade pumpkin puree for this recipe. Make sure it's plain pumpkin puree and not pumpkin pie filling, which has added sugars and spices.
- Storage: Store leftover pumpkin bread in an airtight container at room temperature for up to 3-4 days. It can also be wrapped tightly and frozen for longer storage.
- Variations: Feel free to customize this recipe by adding your favorite spices like ginger or allspice, or swapping out walnuts for pecans or almonds.

This Walnut and Pumpkin Bread is moist, flavorful, and perfect for enjoying during the fall season or any time of the year. Its combination of pumpkin and walnuts makes it a comforting and delicious treat!

Walnut and Apricot Bites

Ingredients:

- 1 cup walnuts
- 1 cup dried apricots (unsweetened if possible)
- 1/2 cup shredded coconut (unsweetened)
- 1 tablespoon honey or maple syrup (optional, for added sweetness)
- 1/2 teaspoon vanilla extract (optional)
- Pinch of salt

Instructions:

1. Prepare Walnuts and Apricots:
   - In a food processor, pulse the walnuts until finely chopped but not powdered. Transfer to a bowl and set aside.
2. Process Apricots:
   - Add the dried apricots to the food processor and pulse until they are finely chopped and start to clump together.
3. Combine Ingredients:
   - Add the chopped walnuts back into the food processor with the apricots. Add shredded coconut, honey or maple syrup (if using), vanilla extract (if using), and a pinch of salt.
4. Process Until Combined:
   - Pulse the mixture in the food processor until everything is well combined and the mixture sticks together when pressed between your fingers. You should have a slightly sticky and cohesive dough.
5. Form Bites:
   - Take small portions of the mixture and roll them into bite-sized balls using your hands. If the mixture is too sticky, dampen your hands with water to prevent sticking.
6. Optional Coating:
   - Roll the bites in additional shredded coconut, cocoa powder, or finely chopped nuts for an extra layer of flavor and texture.
7. Chill (Optional):
   - For firmer bites, place them in the refrigerator for about 30 minutes to set.
8. Serve or Store:
   - Enjoy the Walnut and Apricot Bites immediately, or store them in an airtight container in the refrigerator for up to 1 week.

Tips:

- Variations: Feel free to customize these bites by adding other dried fruits such as dates or figs, or adding spices like cinnamon or nutmeg for extra flavor.

- Nut-Free Option: If you have a nut allergy, you can substitute the walnuts with sunflower seeds or pumpkin seeds.
- Make-Ahead: These bites are perfect for meal prep and can be made ahead of time for a quick and healthy snack throughout the week.

These Walnut and Apricot Bites are not only delicious but also nutritious, providing a good source of fiber, healthy fats, and natural sweetness. They make a great addition to your snack rotation or a wonderful homemade gift!

Walnut and Raspberry Bars

Ingredients:

- For the Crust and Topping:
    - 1 cup all-purpose flour
    - 1/2 cup granulated sugar
    - 1/4 teaspoon salt
    - 1/2 cup cold unsalted butter, cut into small cubes
    - 1/2 cup chopped walnuts
- For the Filling:
    - 1 cup raspberry jam (seedless preferred)
    - 1/2 cup fresh raspberries (optional, for extra texture and flavor)
    - 1/4 cup chopped walnuts

Instructions:

1. Preheat Oven and Prepare Pan:
    - Preheat your oven to 350°F (175°C). Grease or line an 8x8-inch baking pan with parchment paper, leaving some overhang for easy removal.
2. Make the Crust:
    - In a medium bowl, whisk together the flour, sugar, and salt. Add the cold cubed butter and using a pastry cutter or your fingers, work the butter into the dry ingredients until the mixture resembles coarse crumbs.
3. Form the Crust:
    - Reserve about 1/2 cup of the crust mixture for the topping. Press the remaining crust mixture evenly into the bottom of the prepared baking pan.
4. Bake the Crust:
    - Bake the crust in the preheated oven for 15-18 minutes, or until it just starts to turn golden brown around the edges.
5. Prepare the Filling:
    - While the crust is baking, prepare the filling. In a small bowl, mix together the raspberry jam and fresh raspberries (if using) until well combined.
6. Assemble the Bars:
    - Remove the partially baked crust from the oven. Spread the raspberry jam mixture evenly over the warm crust.
7. Add Walnuts and Topping:
    - Sprinkle the chopped walnuts evenly over the raspberry layer.
8. Top with Reserved Crust Mixture:
    - Crumble the reserved 1/2 cup of crust mixture evenly over the top of the raspberry and walnut layers.
9. Bake Again:
    - Return the pan to the oven and bake for an additional 25-30 minutes, or until the top is golden brown and the filling is bubbly around the edges.
10. Cool and Slice:

- Allow the bars to cool completely in the pan on a wire rack. Once cooled, use the parchment paper overhang to lift the bars out of the pan and transfer them to a cutting board. Cut into squares or bars.

11. Serve:
    - Serve the Walnut and Raspberry Bars at room temperature. They can be stored in an airtight container at room temperature for up to 3 days, or refrigerated for longer storage.

Tips:

- Variations: You can substitute the raspberry jam with any other favorite fruit preserves, such as strawberry or apricot.
- Texture: For added texture and freshness, sprinkle a handful of fresh raspberries on top of the jam layer before adding the chopped walnuts.
- Nut-Free Option: If you prefer a nut-free version, you can omit the walnuts or substitute them with oats or additional flour in the crust and topping.

These Walnut and Raspberry Bars are a delightful combination of flavors and textures, making them perfect for a sweet treat or a special occasion dessert. Enjoy the rich nuttiness of the walnuts paired with the fruity sweetness of raspberries in every bite!

Walnut, Date, and Coconut Balls

Ingredients:

- 1 cup pitted dates
- 1 cup walnuts
- 1/2 cup shredded coconut (unsweetened)
- 1 tablespoon coconut oil (optional, for binding)
- Pinch of salt
- Additional shredded coconut, for rolling (optional)

Instructions:

1. Prepare Dates:
   - If your dates are not already soft, soak them in warm water for 10-15 minutes to soften. Drain well before using.
2. Process Walnuts and Dates:
   - In a food processor, pulse the walnuts until finely chopped. Add the pitted dates and pulse until the mixture starts to come together and the dates are finely chopped and incorporated with the walnuts.
3. Add Coconut and Salt:
   - Add the shredded coconut and a pinch of salt to the food processor. Pulse a few more times until everything is well combined.
4. Add Coconut Oil (if using):
   - If the mixture seems dry and doesn't stick together when pressed, add 1 tablespoon of coconut oil to help bind the ingredients. Pulse again until the mixture sticks together and forms a dough-like consistency.
5. Form Balls:
   - Take small portions of the mixture and roll them into bite-sized balls using your hands. If the mixture is too sticky, dampen your hands with water to prevent sticking.
6. Optional: Roll in Coconut:
   - If desired, roll the balls in additional shredded coconut to coat the outside. This adds extra texture and flavor.
7. Chill (Optional):
   - For firmer balls, place them in the refrigerator for about 30 minutes to set.
8. Serve or Store:
   - Enjoy the Walnut, Date, and Coconut Balls immediately, or store them in an airtight container in the refrigerator for up to 1 week. They can also be frozen for longer storage.

Tips:

- Variations: Feel free to customize these energy balls by adding other ingredients such as cocoa powder, chia seeds, or a dash of vanilla extract for extra flavor.

- Nut-Free Option: If you have a nut allergy, you can substitute the walnuts with sunflower seeds or pumpkin seeds.
- Make-Ahead: These balls are perfect for meal prep and can be made ahead of time for a quick and healthy snack throughout the week.

These Walnut, Date, and Coconut Balls are a nutritious and satisfying snack option, providing a good source of energy from natural ingredients. Enjoy their sweet and nutty flavors as a guilt-free treat any time of day!

Honey Walnut Shrimp

Ingredients:

- 1 pound large shrimp, peeled and deveined
- Salt and pepper, to taste
- 1/2 cup cornstarch
- Vegetable oil, for frying

For the Sauce:

- 1/2 cup mayonnaise
- 1/4 cup honey
- 1 tablespoon condensed milk or sweetened condensed milk
- 1 tablespoon lemon juice
- 1/4 cup canned sweetened condensed milk
- 1/2 cup walnuts, toasted

Instructions:

1. Prepare the Shrimp:
    - Season the peeled and deveined shrimp with salt and pepper.
2. Coat Shrimp:
    - Coat each shrimp in cornstarch, shaking off any excess.
3. Fry Shrimp:
    - Heat vegetable oil in a large skillet or wok over medium-high heat. Fry the shrimp in batches until they are golden brown and cooked through, about 2-3 minutes per side. Remove and drain on paper towels.
4. Make the Sauce:
    - In a mixing bowl, whisk together the mayonnaise, honey, condensed milk, and lemon juice until smooth and well combined.
5. Toast Walnuts:
    - In a separate dry skillet, toast the walnuts over medium heat until fragrant and lightly browned, about 3-4 minutes. Stir frequently to prevent burning. Remove from heat and set aside.
6. Combine Shrimp and Sauce:
    - In a large bowl, toss the fried shrimp with the prepared sauce until evenly coated.
7. Serve:
    - Transfer the Honey Walnut Shrimp to a serving platter. Sprinkle toasted walnuts over the top as a garnish.
8. Garnish and Serve:
    - Optionally, garnish with additional toasted walnuts and chopped green onions for added flavor and presentation.

Tips:

- Toasting Walnuts: Toasting the walnuts enhances their flavor and crunchiness. Keep an eye on them as they can quickly burn.
- Adjusting Sweetness: Feel free to adjust the amount of honey or sweetened condensed milk in the sauce to suit your taste preferences.
- Serving Suggestions: Serve Honey Walnut Shrimp with steamed rice or vegetables for a complete meal.

Enjoy making this delicious Honey Walnut Shrimp at home! It's a delightful dish that balances sweet honey with crispy shrimp and crunchy walnuts, perfect for a special dinner or a festive occasion.

Walnut and Cheese Stuffed Dates

Ingredients:

- 12 Medjool dates, pitted
- 1/2 cup soft cheese (such as goat cheese, cream cheese, or blue cheese)
- 1/4 cup walnuts, chopped
- Honey, for drizzling (optional)
- Fresh thyme leaves or rosemary sprigs, for garnish (optional)

Instructions:

1. Prepare Dates:
    - Using a small knife, carefully slice each date lengthwise on one side to create an opening. Remove the pit from each date.
2. Prepare Filling:
    - In a small bowl, mix together the soft cheese and chopped walnuts until well combined.
3. Stuff Dates:
    - Take a small spoonful of the cheese and walnut mixture and stuff it into each date where the pit was removed. Press gently to close the date around the filling.
4. Optional: Drizzle with Honey:
    - If desired, drizzle a little honey over the stuffed dates for extra sweetness.
5. Garnish:
    - Garnish each stuffed date with fresh thyme leaves or a sprig of rosemary for a pop of color and flavor.
6. Serve:
    - Arrange the Walnut and Cheese Stuffed Dates on a serving platter and serve immediately. They can also be chilled for 30 minutes before serving for a slightly firmer texture.

Tips:

- Cheese Options: Experiment with different types of soft cheese such as goat cheese, cream cheese, or even blue cheese for varied flavors.
- Nuts: Substitute walnuts with toasted almonds, pecans, or pistachios for different textures and flavors.
- Sweetness: If you prefer a sweeter version, you can mix a little honey into the cheese filling or drizzle more honey on top of the stuffed dates before serving.

These Walnut and Cheese Stuffed Dates are a wonderful combination of sweet, savory, and crunchy flavors that make them a delightful appetizer or snack for any occasion. Enjoy their deliciousness and simplicity!

Roasted Walnut and Garlic Soup

Ingredients:

- 1 cup walnuts, chopped
- 1 head of garlic
- 2 tablespoons olive oil
- 1 onion, chopped
- 2 celery stalks, chopped
- 2 carrots, chopped
- 4 cups vegetable or chicken broth
- 1/2 teaspoon dried thyme
- Salt and pepper, to taste
- 1/2 cup heavy cream (optional)
- Fresh parsley, chopped, for garnish

Instructions:

1. Roast Garlic:
    - Preheat your oven to 400°F (200°C). Slice off the top of the garlic head to expose the cloves slightly. Drizzle with olive oil, wrap in foil, and roast in the oven for about 30-40 minutes, or until the garlic cloves are soft and golden. Let it cool, then squeeze out the roasted garlic cloves.
2. Toast Walnuts:
    - While the garlic is roasting, spread the chopped walnuts on a baking sheet and toast in the oven for 5-7 minutes, until lightly golden and fragrant. Watch them closely to avoid burning. Set aside.
3. Prepare Vegetables:
    - In a large pot, heat olive oil over medium heat. Add the chopped onion, celery, and carrots. Sauté for about 5-7 minutes, until the vegetables are softened.
4. Combine Ingredients:
    - Add the roasted garlic cloves and toasted walnuts to the pot with the sautéed vegetables. Stir well to combine.
5. Simmer Soup:
    - Pour in the vegetable or chicken broth. Add dried thyme, salt, and pepper to taste. Bring the mixture to a boil, then reduce the heat and let it simmer for about 20-25 minutes, until the vegetables are tender and flavors are melded.
6. Blend Soup:
    - Use an immersion blender to purée the soup until smooth and creamy. Alternatively, transfer the soup in batches to a blender and blend until smooth. Be cautious when blending hot liquids.
7. Finish Soup:
    - Stir in heavy cream, if using, to add richness to the soup. Adjust seasoning with salt and pepper if needed.
8. Serve:

- Ladle the Roasted Walnut and Garlic Soup into bowls. Garnish with chopped fresh parsley and a drizzle of olive oil, if desired. Serve hot and enjoy!

Tips:

- Vegetarian/Vegan Options: Substitute heavy cream with coconut milk or omit it entirely for a dairy-free version.
- Texture: For a chunkier soup, reserve some of the toasted walnuts and stir them into the soup just before serving.
- Storage: Store leftover soup in an airtight container in the refrigerator for up to 3-4 days. Reheat gently on the stove before serving.

This Roasted Walnut and Garlic Soup is creamy, comforting, and full of robust flavors from the roasted walnuts and garlic. It makes a wonderful starter or a light meal paired with crusty bread. Enjoy this unique soup recipe!

Walnut and Avocado Salad

Ingredients:

- 4 cups mixed salad greens (such as spinach, arugula, or mixed baby greens)
- 1 ripe avocado, sliced or diced
- 1/2 cup walnuts, toasted and chopped
- 1/4 cup crumbled feta cheese (optional)
- 1/4 cup dried cranberries or pomegranate arils (optional, for sweetness)
- 1/4 cup red onion, thinly sliced
- 1 tablespoon fresh lemon juice
- 2 tablespoons extra virgin olive oil
- Salt and pepper, to taste

Instructions:

1. Prepare Salad Greens:
   - Wash and dry the salad greens thoroughly. Place them in a large salad bowl or on individual serving plates.
2. Toast Walnuts:
   - In a dry skillet over medium heat, toast the walnuts for 3-5 minutes, stirring frequently, until they are fragrant and lightly browned. Remove from heat and let them cool slightly before chopping.
3. Prepare Avocado:
   - Slice or dice the avocado and gently toss it with lemon juice to prevent browning.
4. Assemble Salad:
   - Arrange the sliced avocado over the salad greens. Sprinkle with toasted walnuts, crumbled feta cheese (if using), dried cranberries or pomegranate arils (if using), and thinly sliced red onion.
5. Make Dressing:
   - In a small bowl, whisk together the extra virgin olive oil, fresh lemon juice, salt, and pepper to taste.
6. Dress Salad:
   - Drizzle the dressing over the salad ingredients. Toss gently to coat everything evenly.
7. Serve:
   - Serve the Walnut and Avocado Salad immediately as a light and refreshing meal or side dish.

Tips:

- Variations: Feel free to customize this salad by adding grilled chicken, shrimp, or tofu for added protein. You can also swap feta cheese with goat cheese or omit it for a vegan option.

- Extra Crunch: For extra crunch, add some crispy bacon bits or croutons to the salad.
- Storage: If making ahead, keep the avocado separate and add just before serving to prevent browning. Store any leftover dressing separately and toss just before serving.

This Walnut and Avocado Salad is not only delicious but also nutritious, providing a good source of healthy fats from walnuts and avocado. Enjoy the combination of textures and flavors in this vibrant salad!

Cinnamon Walnut Pancakes

Ingredients:

- 1 cup all-purpose flour
- 2 tablespoons granulated sugar
- 1 teaspoon baking powder
- 1/2 teaspoon baking soda
- 1/2 teaspoon salt
- 1 teaspoon ground cinnamon
- 1/4 teaspoon ground nutmeg (optional)
- 1 cup buttermilk
- 1 large egg
- 2 tablespoons unsalted butter, melted
- 1 teaspoon vanilla extract
- 1/2 cup chopped walnuts
- Butter or oil for cooking
- Maple syrup, for serving

Instructions:

1. Prepare Dry Ingredients:
    - In a large bowl, whisk together the flour, sugar, baking powder, baking soda, salt, ground cinnamon, and nutmeg (if using).
2. Prepare Wet Ingredients:
    - In another bowl, whisk together the buttermilk, egg, melted butter, and vanilla extract until well combined.
3. Combine Wet and Dry Ingredients:
    - Pour the wet ingredients into the dry ingredients and stir until just combined. Be careful not to overmix; a few lumps are okay. Fold in the chopped walnuts.
4. Heat Griddle or Pan:
    - Heat a non-stick griddle or large skillet over medium heat. Add a small amount of butter or oil and spread it evenly.
5. Cook Pancakes:
    - Pour about 1/4 cup of batter for each pancake onto the heated griddle. Cook until bubbles form on the surface of the pancakes and the edges look set, about 2-3 minutes.
6. Flip and Cook:
    - Carefully flip the pancakes and cook until the other side is golden brown, about 1-2 minutes more. Adjust heat as needed to prevent burning.
7. Serve:
    - Transfer the cooked pancakes to a plate and keep warm. Repeat with the remaining batter, adding more butter or oil to the griddle as needed.
8. Serve Warm:

- Serve the Cinnamon Walnut Pancakes warm, topped with butter and maple syrup. Enjoy!

Tips:

- Buttermilk Substitute: If you don't have buttermilk, you can make a substitute by adding 1 tablespoon of lemon juice or vinegar to 1 cup of milk. Let it sit for 5 minutes before using.
- Variations: For an extra cinnamon flavor, you can add a sprinkle of cinnamon sugar on top of each pancake after flipping.
- Storage: Leftover pancakes can be stored in an airtight container in the refrigerator for up to 3 days or frozen for up to 1 month. Reheat in the toaster or microwave before serving.

These Cinnamon Walnut Pancakes are fluffy, flavorful, and perfect for a comforting breakfast or brunch. The combination of cinnamon and walnuts adds a delicious twist to a classic pancake recipe. Enjoy this delightful treat!

Walnut and Rosemary Crackers

Ingredients:

- 1 cup all-purpose flour
- 1/2 cup walnuts, finely chopped
- 2 tablespoons fresh rosemary, finely chopped (or 1 tablespoon dried rosemary)
- 1/2 teaspoon salt
- 1/4 teaspoon black pepper
- 4 tablespoons cold unsalted butter, cut into small pieces
- 3-4 tablespoons cold water

Instructions:

1. Prepare the Dough:
    - In a large bowl, combine the flour, chopped walnuts, rosemary, salt, and black pepper. Mix well to distribute the ingredients evenly.
2. Add Butter:
    - Add the cold butter pieces to the flour mixture. Use your fingers or a pastry cutter to work the butter into the flour until the mixture resembles coarse crumbs and the butter is well incorporated.
3. Form Dough:
    - Gradually add cold water, 1 tablespoon at a time, mixing with a fork or your hands, until the dough begins to come together. You may not need to use all of the water.
4. Shape Dough:
    - Gather the dough into a ball and flatten it into a disc. Wrap it tightly in plastic wrap and refrigerate for at least 30 minutes (or up to 24 hours) to allow the dough to firm up.
5. Preheat Oven:
    - Preheat your oven to 350°F (175°C). Line a baking sheet with parchment paper.
6. Roll Out Dough:
    - On a lightly floured surface, roll out the chilled dough to about 1/8 inch thickness. Use a rolling pin to ensure even thickness.
7. Cut Crackers:
    - Use a sharp knife or a pizza cutter to cut the rolled-out dough into squares or rectangles of desired size. Prick each cracker with a fork to prevent puffing.
8. Bake:
    - Transfer the cut crackers to the prepared baking sheet, leaving a little space between each cracker. Bake in the preheated oven for 12-15 minutes, or until the edges are golden brown and crisp.
9. Cool and Serve:
    - Remove the crackers from the oven and allow them to cool completely on a wire rack. Once cooled, store in an airtight container at room temperature.

Tips:

- Variations: You can customize these crackers by adding other herbs like thyme or sage, or even a sprinkle of Parmesan cheese for extra flavor.
- Storage: These crackers will keep well in an airtight container at room temperature for up to 1 week. They can also be frozen for longer storage.
- Serve With: Enjoy these Walnut and Rosemary Crackers with your favorite cheese, hummus, or dips for a delicious appetizer or snack.

These homemade Walnut and Rosemary Crackers are crisp, flavorful, and perfect for any occasion. They're sure to impress with their nutty crunch and aromatic rosemary essence. Enjoy making and sharing these savory crackers!

Walnut and Orange Cake

Ingredients:

- 1 cup walnuts, finely chopped
- 1 cup unsalted butter, softened
- 1 cup granulated sugar
- 4 large eggs
- 2 cups all-purpose flour
- 2 teaspoons baking powder
- 1/2 teaspoon salt
- Zest of 2 oranges
- Juice of 1 orange
- 1 teaspoon vanilla extract
- Powdered sugar, for dusting (optional)

Instructions:

1. Prepare the Walnuts:
   - Preheat your oven to 350°F (175°C). Spread the chopped walnuts on a baking sheet and toast in the oven for about 5-7 minutes, or until fragrant. Remove from the oven and let them cool.
2. Prepare the Batter:
   - In a large mixing bowl, cream together the softened butter and granulated sugar until light and fluffy.
3. Add Eggs and Flavorings:
   - Add the eggs one at a time, beating well after each addition. Stir in the vanilla extract, orange zest, and orange juice.
4. Combine Dry Ingredients:
   - In a separate bowl, whisk together the flour, baking powder, and salt.
5. Incorporate Ingredients:
   - Gradually add the dry ingredients to the wet ingredients, mixing until just combined. Fold in the toasted walnuts until evenly distributed in the batter.
6. Bake the Cake:
   - Grease and flour a 9-inch round cake pan or a loaf pan. Pour the batter into the prepared pan and smooth the top with a spatula.
7. Bake in the Oven:
   - Bake in the preheated oven for 40-45 minutes, or until a toothpick inserted into the center comes out clean. The top should be golden brown and spring back when lightly pressed.
8. Cool and Serve:
   - Allow the cake to cool in the pan for about 10 minutes, then transfer it to a wire rack to cool completely. Dust with powdered sugar before serving, if desired.

Tips:

- Orange Glaze: For an extra burst of orange flavor, you can prepare a simple glaze by mixing powdered sugar with orange juice and drizzling it over the cooled cake.
- Variations: You can add a handful of dried cranberries or raisins to the batter for added texture and sweetness.
- Storage: Store the Walnut and Orange Cake in an airtight container at room temperature for up to 3 days, or refrigerate for longer freshness.

This Walnut and Orange Cake is a wonderful blend of nuttiness and citrus that is sure to please your taste buds. Enjoy it with a cup of tea or coffee for a delightful treat!

Spicy Walnut and Olive Tapenade

Ingredients:

- 1 cup walnuts, toasted
- 1 cup pitted Kalamata olives
- 2 cloves garlic, minced
- 1 teaspoon capers, drained
- 1 tablespoon fresh lemon juice
- 1 teaspoon lemon zest
- 1/2 teaspoon red pepper flakes (adjust to taste)
- 1/4 cup extra virgin olive oil
- Salt and black pepper, to taste

Instructions:

1. Toast Walnuts:
    - Preheat your oven to 350°F (175°C). Spread the walnuts on a baking sheet and toast in the oven for about 5-7 minutes, or until fragrant and lightly browned. Remove and let them cool.
2. Prepare Tapenade:
    - In a food processor, combine the toasted walnuts, pitted Kalamata olives, minced garlic, capers, lemon juice, lemon zest, and red pepper flakes.
3. Pulse to Combine:
    - Pulse the ingredients until coarsely chopped and well combined. Scrape down the sides of the food processor as needed.
4. Drizzle Olive Oil:
    - With the food processor running, gradually drizzle in the extra virgin olive oil until the mixture becomes a thick paste. Continue blending until desired consistency is reached. You may not need to use all of the olive oil.
5. Season:
    - Taste and season the tapenade with salt and black pepper, adjusting to your preference.
6. Serve:
    - Transfer the Spicy Walnut and Olive Tapenade to a serving bowl. Serve immediately or refrigerate for at least 30 minutes to allow the flavors to meld.
7. Enjoy:
    - Serve the tapenade as a spread on bread or crackers, a dip for vegetables, or as a flavorful topping for grilled meats or fish.

Tips:

- Storage: Store any leftover tapenade in an airtight container in the refrigerator for up to one week. Bring to room temperature before serving.

- Variations: For a milder flavor, you can use green olives or a mix of green and Kalamata olives. Adjust the amount of red pepper flakes to suit your spice preference.
- Uses: This tapenade also makes a delicious topping for pasta, pizzas, or as a condiment in sandwiches.

This Spicy Walnut and Olive Tapenade is a versatile and delicious addition to your appetizer repertoire, combining the rich nuttiness of walnuts with the briny saltiness of olives and a kick of spice. Enjoy its robust flavors on any occasion!

Walnut and Carrot Cake

Ingredients:

- 2 cups all-purpose flour
- 1 teaspoon baking powder
- 1 teaspoon baking soda
- 1/2 teaspoon salt
- 1 teaspoon ground cinnamon
- 1/2 teaspoon ground nutmeg
- 1/2 teaspoon ground ginger
- 1 cup granulated sugar
- 1 cup light brown sugar, packed
- 1 cup vegetable oil or melted coconut oil
- 4 large eggs, at room temperature
- 2 teaspoons vanilla extract
- 3 cups grated carrots (about 3-4 medium carrots)
- 1 cup walnuts, chopped (plus extra for garnish, optional)
- Cream cheese frosting (see recipe below)

Cream Cheese Frosting:

- 8 oz (225g) cream cheese, softened
- 1/2 cup (115g) unsalted butter, softened
- 3-4 cups powdered sugar
- 1 teaspoon vanilla extract

Instructions:

1. Prepare the Cake Batter:
    - Preheat your oven to 350°F (175°C). Grease and flour two 9-inch round cake pans or line them with parchment paper.
2. Mix Dry Ingredients:
    - In a large bowl, whisk together the flour, baking powder, baking soda, salt, cinnamon, nutmeg, and ginger until well combined. Set aside.
3. Combine Wet Ingredients:
    - In another large bowl, beat together the granulated sugar, brown sugar, and vegetable oil until smooth. Add the eggs one at a time, mixing well after each addition. Stir in the vanilla extract.
4. Combine Wet and Dry Mixtures:
    - Gradually add the dry ingredients to the wet ingredients, mixing until just combined. Do not overmix. Fold in the grated carrots and chopped walnuts until evenly distributed in the batter.
5. Bake the Cake:

- Divide the batter evenly between the prepared cake pans. Smooth the tops with a spatula. Bake in the preheated oven for 25-30 minutes, or until a toothpick inserted into the center comes out clean.
6. Cool the Cakes:
   - Remove the cakes from the oven and let them cool in the pans for about 10 minutes. Then, carefully transfer them to a wire rack to cool completely.
7. Prepare the Cream Cheese Frosting:
   - In a mixing bowl, beat the softened cream cheese and butter until smooth and creamy. Add the powdered sugar, one cup at a time, beating well after each addition. Stir in the vanilla extract until combined.
8. Assemble the Cake:
   - Once the cakes are completely cooled, place one cake layer on a serving plate or cake stand. Spread a layer of cream cheese frosting evenly over the top. Place the second cake layer on top and frost the top and sides of the cake with the remaining frosting.
9. Garnish and Serve:
   - Optionally, garnish the cake with additional chopped walnuts on top. Slice and serve the Walnut and Carrot Cake, and enjoy!

Tips:

- Storage: Store the frosted cake in an airtight container in the refrigerator for up to 5 days. Bring to room temperature before serving.
- Variations: You can add raisins or shredded coconut to the batter for added texture and sweetness.
- Decoration: For a decorative touch, press whole walnuts into the sides of the frosted cake.

This Walnut and Carrot Cake is moist, flavorful, and perfect for any celebration or gathering. The combination of carrots, walnuts, and warm spices makes it a beloved classic. Enjoy baking and savoring this delicious cake!

Walnut and Lemon Biscotti

Ingredients:

- 2 cups all-purpose flour
- 1 cup granulated sugar
- 1 teaspoon baking powder
- 1/2 teaspoon salt
- Zest of 2 lemons
- 1 cup walnuts, coarsely chopped
- 3 large eggs
- 1 teaspoon vanilla extract
- 2 tablespoons fresh lemon juice

Instructions:

1. Preheat Oven:
   - Preheat your oven to 350°F (175°C). Line a baking sheet with parchment paper or a silicone baking mat.
2. Mix Dry Ingredients:
   - In a large bowl, whisk together the flour, sugar, baking powder, salt, and lemon zest.
3. Add Walnuts:
   - Stir in the chopped walnuts until evenly distributed in the flour mixture.
4. Combine Wet Ingredients:
   - In a separate bowl, whisk together the eggs, vanilla extract, and fresh lemon juice until well combined.
5. Form Dough:
   - Pour the wet ingredients into the dry ingredients and stir with a wooden spoon or spatula until a dough forms. The dough will be slightly sticky.
6. Shape the Biscotti:
   - Transfer the dough onto a lightly floured surface. Divide the dough in half. Shape each half into a log about 12 inches long and 2 inches wide. Place the logs on the prepared baking sheet, spacing them apart.
7. Bake First Time:
   - Bake in the preheated oven for 25-30 minutes, or until the logs are firm to the touch and lightly golden brown.
8. Cool and Slice:
   - Remove the baking sheet from the oven and let the logs cool for 10-15 minutes. Reduce the oven temperature to 325°F (160°C).
9. Slice Biscotti:
   - Using a serrated knife, carefully slice the logs diagonally into 1/2-inch thick slices. Arrange the slices cut-side down on the baking sheet.
10. Second Bake:

- Bake the sliced biscotti for an additional 15-20 minutes, turning them halfway through baking, until they are crisp and golden brown. The longer you bake them, the crispier they will become.
11. Cool Completely:
    - Transfer the biscotti to a wire rack to cool completely. They will continue to crisp up as they cool.
12. Serve or Store:
    - Once cooled, store the Walnut and Lemon Biscotti in an airtight container at room temperature. Enjoy them dipped in coffee, tea, or on their own as a delicious treat!

Tips:

- Variations: You can add a drizzle of melted white or dark chocolate over the cooled biscotti for an extra touch of sweetness.
- Storage: Biscotti can be stored in an airtight container at room temperature for up to 2 weeks. They also freeze well for longer storage.
- Gift Idea: Packaged in a decorative tin or box, these biscotti make a lovely homemade gift for friends and family.

Enjoy baking and savoring these Walnut and Lemon Biscotti with their delightful blend of flavors and satisfying crunch!

Walnut and Herb Stuffed Tomatoes

Ingredients:

- 4 large tomatoes
- 1 cup walnuts, finely chopped
- 1/2 cup fresh breadcrumbs
- 1/4 cup grated Parmesan cheese
- 2 cloves garlic, minced
- 2 tablespoons fresh parsley, chopped
- 1 tablespoon fresh basil, chopped
- 1 tablespoon fresh thyme leaves (or 1 teaspoon dried thyme)
- Salt and pepper, to taste
- 3 tablespoons extra virgin olive oil, divided
- Optional: additional grated Parmesan cheese for topping

Instructions:

1. Prepare the Tomatoes:
    - Preheat your oven to 375°F (190°C). Slice off the tops of the tomatoes and scoop out the seeds and pulp with a spoon, leaving a hollow shell. Season the inside of the tomatoes with a pinch of salt and pepper. Place them in a baking dish.
2. Make the Filling:
    - In a mixing bowl, combine the chopped walnuts, breadcrumbs, grated Parmesan cheese, minced garlic, chopped parsley, basil, thyme, salt, and pepper. Drizzle 2 tablespoons of olive oil over the mixture and toss to combine until the filling is evenly moistened.
3. Stuff the Tomatoes:
    - Spoon the walnut and herb mixture into the hollowed-out tomatoes, pressing gently to pack the filling.
4. Bake the Stuffed Tomatoes:
    - Drizzle the remaining tablespoon of olive oil over the stuffed tomatoes. Optionally, sprinkle with additional grated Parmesan cheese for extra flavor.
    - Bake in the preheated oven for 25-30 minutes, or until the tomatoes are tender and the filling is golden brown and crispy on top.
5. Serve Warm:
    - Remove the stuffed tomatoes from the oven and let them cool slightly before serving. Garnish with additional fresh herbs if desired.

Tips:

- Variations: You can add diced cooked chicken, quinoa, or rice to the filling for added protein.

- Make-Ahead: You can prepare the stuffed tomatoes in advance and refrigerate them, covered, until ready to bake.
- Serve With: These Walnut and Herb Stuffed Tomatoes are delicious served alongside a salad or as a side dish to grilled meats or fish.

Enjoy these Walnut and Herb Stuffed Tomatoes as a flavorful and nutritious addition to your meal!

Walnut and Chocolate Truffles

Ingredients:

- 8 oz (225g) dark chocolate (60-70% cocoa), finely chopped
- 1/2 cup heavy cream
- 1 cup walnuts, finely chopped
- Cocoa powder, powdered sugar, or finely chopped walnuts for rolling (optional)

Instructions:

1. Prepare the Chocolate Ganache:
    - Place the finely chopped dark chocolate in a heatproof bowl.
    - In a small saucepan, heat the heavy cream over medium heat until it just begins to simmer (do not boil). Remove from heat immediately.
    - Pour the hot cream over the chopped chocolate. Let it sit undisturbed for 1-2 minutes to allow the chocolate to soften.
2. Mix the Ganache:
    - Gently stir the chocolate and cream mixture with a spatula or whisk until the chocolate is completely melted and the mixture is smooth and shiny.
3. Add Chopped Walnuts:
    - Stir in the finely chopped walnuts until evenly distributed in the chocolate ganache.
4. Chill the Mixture:
    - Cover the bowl with plastic wrap and refrigerate the mixture for at least 2 hours, or until firm enough to scoop.
5. Shape the Truffles:
    - Once chilled, use a spoon or a small cookie scoop to scoop out portions of the chocolate ganache mixture. Roll each portion into a smooth ball between your palms. If the mixture is too sticky, lightly dust your hands with cocoa powder.
6. Roll in Coatings (Optional):
    - Roll the truffles in cocoa powder, powdered sugar, or finely chopped walnuts for coating. Place the coated truffles on a baking sheet lined with parchment paper.
7. Chill Again (Optional):
    - If the truffles have softened during shaping, chill them in the refrigerator for 15-20 minutes to firm up before serving.
8. Serve and Enjoy:
    - Serve the Walnut and Chocolate Truffles at room temperature. Store any leftover truffles in an airtight container in the refrigerator for up to 1 week.

Tips:

- Variations: For extra flavor, you can add a splash of vanilla extract or a tablespoon of your favorite liqueur (such as rum, brandy, or amaretto) to the chocolate ganache mixture before chilling.

- Decoration: Before the truffles set completely, you can garnish them with a walnut half or a sprinkle of sea salt for an elegant touch.
- Gift Idea: Pack these Walnut and Chocolate Truffles in a decorative box or tin for a thoughtful homemade gift.

These Walnut and Chocolate Truffles are rich, decadent, and sure to impress with their combination of smooth chocolate and crunchy walnuts. Enjoy making and sharing these delightful treats!

Walnut and Banana Smoothie

Ingredients:

- 1 ripe banana, peeled and sliced
- 1/4 cup walnuts, chopped
- 1 cup unsweetened almond milk (or any milk of your choice)
- 1 tablespoon honey or maple syrup (optional, for added sweetness)
- 1/2 teaspoon ground cinnamon (optional, for extra flavor)
- Ice cubes (optional, for a chilled smoothie)

Instructions:

1. Prepare Ingredients:
   - Peel and slice the ripe banana. Chop the walnuts into smaller pieces.
2. Blend Ingredients:
   - In a blender, combine the sliced banana, chopped walnuts, almond milk, honey or maple syrup (if using), and ground cinnamon (if using).
3. Blend Until Smooth:
   - Blend on high speed until the mixture is smooth and creamy. If you prefer a thicker smoothie, add fewer ice cubes or omit them altogether.
4. Adjust Consistency (Optional):
   - If the smoothie is too thick, add a little more almond milk. If it's too thin, add a few more walnuts or banana slices.
5. Serve:
   - Pour the Walnut and Banana Smoothie into glasses. Optionally, garnish with a sprinkle of ground cinnamon or a few chopped walnuts on top.
6. Enjoy Immediately:
   - Serve the smoothie immediately while it's fresh and chilled.

Tips:

- Variations: You can add a tablespoon of chia seeds or flax seeds for added fiber and nutrients. Additionally, you can include a scoop of protein powder for a more filling smoothie.
- Nutritional Boost: Consider adding a handful of spinach or kale for extra vitamins and minerals without altering the flavor significantly.
- Storage: It's best to enjoy the smoothie immediately after blending. However, you can store any leftovers in a sealed container in the refrigerator for up to 1 day.

This Walnut and Banana Smoothie is not only delicious but also packed with protein, healthy fats, and potassium from the walnuts and banana. It's a fantastic way to start your day or to recharge in the afternoon!